the About.com guide to
HOME
DECORATING

A Room-by-Room Guide to Creating the House of Your Dreams

Coral Nafie with Barbara Cameron

Adams Media
Avon, Massachusetts

About About.com

About.com is a powerful network of more than 600 Guides—smart, passionate, accomplished people who are experts in their fields. About.com Guides live and work in more than twenty countries and celebrate their interests in thousands of topics. They have written books, appeared on national television programs, and won many awards in their fields. Guides are selected for their ability to provide the most interesting information for users and for their passion for their subject and the Web. The selection process is rigorous—only 2 percent of those who apply actually become Guides. The following are the most important criteria by which they are chosen:

- High level of knowledge and passion for their topic
- Appropriate credentials
- Keen understanding of the Web experience
- Commitment to creating informative, inspiring features

Each month more than 55 million people visit About.com. Whether you need home-repair and decorating ideas, recipes, movie trailers, or car-buying tips, About.com Guides offer practical advice and solutions for everyday life. If you're looking for how-to advice on refinishing your deck, for instance, About.com shows you the tools you need to get the job done. No matter where you are on About.com or how you got there, you'll always find exactly what you're looking for!

3 1907 00201 2838

About Your Guide

 Coral Nafie's decorating experience began when she helped choose the wallpaper and carpet for her childhood bedroom. It's no surprise that she has worked to create many beautiful rooms since then. Each of her own homes has inspired numerous opportunities for painting, wallpapering, choosing flooring, and making window treatments and bedding.

With over twenty-five years of professional experience in home decorating, she has worked on projects in apartments, condominiums, churches, offices, bungalows, mansions, and fabulous designer show houses. As a hands-on decorator with access to designer resources, she has been responsible for designing, buying, fabricating, and installing window and wall treatments and **soft goods** in addition to overseeing every aspect of redecoration, from **budget** makeovers to more extensive renovations.

Coral began writing about home decorating on About.com in March 2004. There she enjoys sharing ideas and resources and offering practical solutions to home decorating challenges. Through the wonders of the Internet, she communicates her interest in home decorating to people around the world.

Acknowledgments

My parents encouraged me at every stage of my life, and I feel their inspiration still. My two beautiful daughters, Anne and Sara, are my best cheerleaders, and I am grateful for how they enrich every day of my life. My siblings and their spouses believe in me and offer tremendous support. About.com allows me to share my interests with the world.

This book would not have been written without the tireless work of Barbara Cameron, and I offer her my sincere thanks.

ABOUT.COM

CEO & President
Scott Meyer

COO
Andrew Pancer

SVP Content
Michael Daecher

Director, About Operations
Chris Murphy

Marketing Communications Manager
Lisa Langsdorf

ADAMS MEDIA

Editorial

Publishing Director
Gary M. Krebs

Managing Editor
Laura M. Daly

Executive Editor
Brielle K. Matson

Development Editor
Katie McDonough

Marketing

Director of Marketing
Karen Cooper

Assistant Art Director
Frank Rivera

Production

Director of Manufacturing
Susan Beale

Production Project Manager
Michelle Roy Kelly

Senior Book Designer
Colleen Cunningham

Copyright ©2007, F+W Publications, Inc.

About.com® is a registered trademark of About, Inc.

Published by Adams Media, an F+W Publications Company
57 Littlefield Street
Avon, MA 02322
www.adamsmedia.com

ISBN-10: 1-59869-347-6
ISBN-13: 978-1-59869-347-8

Printed in China.

J I H G F E D C B A

Library of Congress Cataloging-in-Publication Data
is available from the publisher.

This publication is designed to provide accurate and authoritative information with regard to the subject matter covered. It is sold with the understanding that the publisher is not engaged in rendering legal, accounting, or other professional advice. If legal advice or other expert assistance is required, the services of a competent professional person should be sought.
—From a *Declaration of Principles* jointly adopted by a Committee of the American Bar Association and a Committee of Publishers and Associations

Many of the designations used by manufacturers and sellers to distinguish their product are claimed as trademarks. Where those designations appear in this book and Adams Media was aware of a trademark claim, the designations have been printed with initial capital letters.

Interior photos Copyright © Brand X Pictures, © Digistock

Interior illustrations by Eric Andrews

This book is available at quantity discounts for bulk purchases. For information, please call 1-800-289-0963.

How to Use This Book

Each About.com book is written by an About.com Guide—a specialist with expert knowledge of his or her subject. Although the book can stand on its own as a helpful resource, it may also be coupled with its corresponding About.com site for further tips, tools, and advice. Each book not only refers you back to About.com but also directs you to other useful Internet locations and print resources.

All About.com books include a special section at the end of each chapter called Get Linked. There you'll find a few links back to the About.com site for even more useful information on the topics discussed in that chapter. Depending on the topic, you will find links to such resources as photos, sheet music, quizzes, recipes, or product reviews.

About.com books also include four types of sidebars:

- **Ask Your Guide:** Detailed information in a question-and-answer format
- **Tools You Need:** Advice about researching, purchasing, and using a variety of tools for your projects
- **Elsewhere on the Web:** References to other useful Internet locations
- **What's Hot:** All you need to know about the hottest trends and tips out there

Each About.com book takes you on a personal tour of a certain topic, gives you reliable advice, and leaves you with the knowledge you need to achieve your goals.

CONTENTS

CONTENTS . . . *continued*

Introduction from Your Guide

If you love inhabiting a beautiful home, you'll want to learn as much as you can about decorating the spaces you live in. I'll lead you through the process of making your home comfortable, beautiful, and functional for your individual lifestyle.

My first piece of advice is to have fun. Of course, work is involved. Nothing that is worthwhile comes easily. But there are some projects that are difficult and some that are less challenging. This book will help you take on those projects you feel comfortable with and advise you on when you should engage the expertise of a professional.

Most of us don't have a sky-high budget to turn our home into the place of our dreams. However, there are things we can all do to make our home more inviting, more personal, and more of a comfort. The pages of this book will guide you through the process of identifying problem areas, provide solutions to challenges, and help you decide on the best course of action.

Whether you're traditional or trendy, you have to decide. Only you know the answer. Creating a home that reflects your taste, your budget, and your lifestyle will allow you to enjoy your personal time more.

Perhaps you are able to picture exactly what you want at the outset. You may know instinctively which style is right for you and which is not. Or you may not have a clue and your decorating decisions will reflect your growing enlightenment. You'll start with a vague image that will come into focus as you become more involved in the process.

Certain areas of your home, like your bedroom and bathroom, are your own private spaces and they should reflect exactly what you want. Whether you decide on a warm sanctuary or a contemporary, uncluttered space, you are usually the boss here.

With other spaces that are less private, you might need to compromise a bit. Even if you have your bed in the living room, you know you need seating and lighting for when friends come to visit. Nevertheless, you can use this more public space to display pieces that are special to you so that the room reflects your individuality and personal history. Refrain from following conventional designs and allow your rooms to be original and uncontrived.

As you embark on this road to creating a more beautiful home, look around you. Get rid of what you don't like and what you don't need. Clear away or pack away anything that will not have a place in your new plan. Analyze the bare bones of your space and decide how you use it, whether for work, dining, entertaining, or relaxing. Determine how many people will use the space and when. Find the perfect place for objects that are special. Locate resources for wall coverings or paint, fabrics, flooring, and accessories. Decide what you can do by yourself and what you'll need to have done for you. Start to collect ideas. You're on your way!

For more inspiration and help, be sure to visit my About.com site at http://interiordec.about.com. I add information, links, and tips almost every day. If you need some individualized help, write to me at *interiordec.guide@about.com*. Although I can't give specific advice, I'll try to guide you to new and helpful resources.

Chapter 1

Why Decorate?

Restless for a Change

No matter how much you might love the furnishings and décor you originally chose for your home, there will probably come a time when you grow tired of your surroundings. People's tastes and styles change with time, and even if yours haven't, it's natural to want a change of scenery every so often. If it's been a while since you refreshed the look of your home, now is a good time to reconsider it.

And maybe you're not only tired of the way things look but also of the way the place feels. You might have noticed that your home isn't as well laid out or as functional as it could be. Do you find that your furniture arrangement isn't conducive to easy traffic flow? Do you have trouble seating all your guests when you have company? Do the kids keep knocking over valuable objects or bumping their heads on that end table with the sharp corners? There's no reason why you should have to live with these nuisances. It's your home,

I'm tired of the way my home looks, but I don't know where to start. Can you help me?

▶ My advice is to start with one room, not the whole house. What bothers you about it? Is it the wall color? The curtains? The furniture? Some things, like an old sofa, can be given new life with very little effort or expense. Try a sofa cover. I've found many stylish ones that make a sofa look new for very little money. The fact that they're usually machine-washable is a plus, too, especially if you have kids or pets.

and you can change things around as much and as often as you want—and it doesn't have to break the bank.

If you're dying to redecorate your home but feel that it might be too big a task for you to handle, put such an intimidating thought out of your mind. You don't have to be an expert with insider resources to achieve your goal. Simple changes like a fresh coat of paint on the wall or a slipcover for the sofa can make a world of difference. Changing out old art and photos for updated ones can give your home a whole new look with minimal effort. And there's no use worrying that you'll make mistakes along the way. (You will.) The important thing to remember is that no change has to be permanent. Paint can be painted over. Fabric can be replaced. Prints and paintings can be returned.

All you need to do is commit to your project, think about what you want, and then take the plunge. This book will be your guide from start to finish, and you have numerous resources to help you along the way. Just start small, be prepared to make adjustments, and—most important—enjoy the process. Decorating can be a lot of fun if you don't let it stress you out.

Renovation

Maybe you're ready to make some structural changes in your home. Perhaps you'd like to take out a wall between rooms and make your space more of an open floor plan. Or you've finally decided that you're going to stay where you are and add on instead of going through the hassle of finding another house—and paying high house prices. Extra square footage will raise the value of your house as well as make it more inviting for you and your family.

As you can imagine, home renovation is a much bigger undertaking than just a matter of redecorating. Such a project shouldn't be daunting, but it does require careful thought, planning, and making a substantial financial investment. Deciding which work to do and how you'll do it is as important as the original decision you made to buy your home.

Just how big is your renovation project? Is it something you can tackle alone or with a friend or family member? Do you have the time? The energy? Does the project involve electrical work? If you're not a licensed electrician, you could be wading into dangerous territory. Before you tear down that wall, do you know if it's a load-bearing wall?

And what about **building permits**? If you need permits but don't get them, you might experience problems later when you go to sell the house and an inspector notes that work has been done incorrectly. Getting a permit before you start guarantees not just the practical reliability of the construction but also partially covers your legal liability. Are you allowed to make this improvement on your own or do you need a licensed **contractor**? Homeowner's insurance may not pay if you cause a fire or a pipe breaks and spews water everywhere, causing damage.

It's important to get several estimates for each component of the renovation and to talk with the professional involved. Not only will you gain a better idea of what kind of financial investment you'll be making, you may also get a different perspective on how to go about a particular renovation.

A general contractor (GC) can make the renovation process go more smoothly. If you've never done a home renovation project before, you'll probably want the help of a GC. A GC is a professional who studies the plans for your renovation project, then gathers the materials and the subcontractors needed for the job.

General contractors have not only trained for every aspect of the job, they are required to take an exam to be licensed. But

WHAT'S HOT

▶ Great rooms have become very popular. This open-style floor plan allows members of a family to interact while one person cooks and others either sit at a kitchen island doing homework or watch television in the living room. Taking down a nonweight-bearing wall or opening up a pass-through in a wall that can't be removed will create a great room. Sometimes just removing cupboards that block visibility into another room will work.

don't just rely on licensing. Ask for references and call every one of them. Call your **Better Business Bureau** to see whether there have been any complaints filed against the contractors you're planning to interview.

Never be afraid to ask a contractor to show you his license and insurance paperwork. He shouldn't be insulted—be wary if he is or shows any hesitation. Your pocketbook and your peace of mind are too important, not to mention the fact that you are legally liable if anyone is hurt on your property or this individual takes off with your money without doing repairs. You should do everything you can to protect yourself.

A general contractor can:

- Translate and interpret architectural plans.
- Schedule all the work and coordinate the timing.
- Locate materials and often get a builder's discount for you.
- Line up and hire all the specialists (such as plumbers, electricians, and **drywall** installers), supervise them, and pay them.
- Maintain a safe working environment.

A general contractor can't:

- Read your mind. Be very clear about what you want and always put it in writing.
- Always get permits for the job. In a few states, this has to be done by the property owner. Check local rules.
- Tell you how much your property will be worth after the improvement.
- Act as your representative to your home insurance company if he's repairing damage.
- Always do the work himself.

It's a good idea to create a timeline. You've heard it so many times: Plan on the renovation project taking twice as long and costing three times as much as estimated. You may be pleasantly surprised, but consider yourself warned!

Always factor in extra time if the renovation needs to be completed by a specific deadline, like for a family reunion at your house for the holidays. You shouldn't have to cancel Thanksgiving or Christmas dinner because the site is still a mess.

Construction and renovation experts will also tell you that you never know exactly what you're getting into until you're in the midst of the project. Taking down drywall may reveal wood rot, water damage, mold—or a structural or safety problem. Even the most careful of measurements may fall short and you suddenly need more tile or wood.

Costs can soar, too, if materials suddenly become scarce, which has happened in some areas after major hurricanes or other natural disasters. Plan for extra time and funds. You know they're going to be needed.

Decorating for Home Sale

Among the many reasons to decorate a home is to get it ready to sell. A house will just not seem desirable to potential buyers if it has peeling, outdated wallpaper, beat-up furniture, and myriad other rough spots. Sometimes you have the luxury of waiting for a buyer who doesn't mind these details, but if you have a deadline to sell because a job is waiting in another location or you want your children to start a different school in the fall, watching potential buyers walk away again and again can pose a real problem. Luckily, there are some relatively simple, inexpensive changes you can make that will make a world of difference to the people who come to look at your home.

First, declutter. Almost everyone just has too much stuff! Even if you don't think all that stuff is messy, it makes your rooms seem smaller. Buyers want to get the most square footage they can, which they'll believe they're getting if rooms are, well, roomy.

Start by taking down fussy, complicated window treatments that clutter a window and block that all-important view. If you have bookcases and display shelves, pack away some of those books and decorative items for a cleaner, simpler look. Clear surfaces such as countertops, the dining room table, and the coffee table. This will help the place look neat and tidy. If you have an area or a room dedicated to a home office, put away papers, magazines, and bills.

You may be hesitant to get rid of or hide so many of your personal touches, but it's important to remember that you're trying to appeal to potential buyers, not your friends and family. Yes, it's your home, and you've spent a lot of time putting your personality into it. But you're selling it now, and other people don't necessarily share your taste or love your decorating style.

Rethink your space. Is your furniture arranged in the "You're under arrest!" style of decorating, where all pieces are located up against the wall? If so, it's probably time to rethink where the furniture is placed.

Walk around the room. Is there a good flow? Can you move easily without bumping into things? There should be a clear pathway between the door and its adjoining room.

Find the room's **focal point**. Is it a fireplace? Entertainment center? Arrange your furniture so that it's logical for you to sit on the sofa and view the fireplace or the television—or both. Consider different arrangements such as angling the sofa or positioning chairs in an area for conversation. Or try making a reading area with an easy chair, an ottoman, and a good lamp.

ELSEWHERE ON THE WEB

▶ An increasing number of network television shows, such as HGTV's *Designed to Sell* and A&E's *Sell This House*, help viewers learn how to get their homes ready to sell. Check out these networks' respective Web sites at www.hgtv.com and www.aetv.com for information about the shows, good tips to try in your own home, and fun features like photo galleries and message boards.

Where should you spend your money? Kitchens and bathrooms are the two rooms that homebuyers consider most important. Money spent there usually produces a huge return—double, triple, sometimes even more than what you've spent. You may have become habituated to dated appliances or outmoded design in the kitchen. Remember that prospective buyers are seeing your house with fresh eyes and need to picture themselves cooking a meal in that kitchen.

Replace what you can and, if money is tight, look into products for painting old appliance surfaces. No money for new kitchen cabinets? Maybe they don't really need to be replaced, just painted or refreshed with stylish new handles. And get rid of anything that looks dated, whether carpeting, linoleum, or cheap-looking tile. Unless yours is a retro house, don't let it show its age!

It's also important to know what not to do. Have you overheard negative comments from realtors or people touring your home? While you can't please everyone, especially those who try to get the most home they can for the least amount of money, you can learn from their comments.

Have you overheard people say they disliked the wallpaper, thought the carpeting looked worn, or noticed the grout on the tiled kitchen counter looked dirty? Consider fixing such eyesores and a sale might be on the way.

Pets can be a problem. Often a pet owner doesn't notice the puppy stains on the carpet or the bowls of food and water that have to be stepped around. And odors? You say you don't smell anything? Ask a friend to be honest with you, and then listen to her. Perhaps you need to do some cleaning and odor control, even find a place for Fluffy to stay while potential homebuyers are touring the house.

And finally, let's talk toys—grown-up toys and kid toys. If you have a big-screen television and a lot of audio equipment that between them take up half the living or family room, consider putting these in storage until the house is sold. If you have small children and their toys are everywhere, the house won't look roomy or orderly. Get rid of some of the toys and contain the rest.

Decorating Before You Move In

Similar to decorating to sell a home is decorating before you move into a new place. Since you will still have a lot of decorating work ahead of you, you want to keep the agenda simple at this early stage. The period when your belongings are still on the moving truck offers a good opportunity to do some basic decorating before you fill the house with furnishings.

For starters, painting an empty room without having to move out rugs and maneuver around plastic-protected furniture speeds up the process. This is also a good time to patch any holes and clean up or repaint baseboards and woodwork around windows and doorways. You'll feel accomplished and have a fresh, clean base from which to work by the time you move the furniture in.

If you want to change light fixtures, doorknobs, or other details, now is the time. You'll have a wide-open workspace for the project and less to worry about once the furniture is in. Also determine whether you need new plates for outlets and light switches. These are quick and inexpensive to replace, and they can go a long way toward making a room look finished.

Finally, if you feel like tackling a bigger project before moving in, such as replacing the kitchen countertop or putting in new carpeting, afterwards you'll probably be glad you did. Just keep in mind your general decorating plan so you don't accidentally choose a style that will clash with what you're bringing in. Making sure your

ELSEWHERE ON THE WEB

▶ Want to find a better way to arrange the furniture in a room? Before you enlist the help of a couple of male family members—or attempt it yourself—try out the hints on how to arrange furniture on Web sites like www.mar thastewart.com and www .bhg.com (the *Better Homes & Gardens* site). For instance, Martha Stewart advises using painter's tape to block off spaces for the sofa and other furniture before you strain your muscles to lift these, and *Better Homes & Gardens* advises using graph paper and other aids.

house is as ready for you as possible by the time you move in will mean a lot less frustration and effort later on.

You Can Do It!

No longer do home projects have to be turned over to outside experts. With the many resources available to you today, you can tackle many jobs you never thought you could. If you've never held a paintbrush, you might be pleasantly surprised at what you can do. Out of a desire to save money by sewing some simple **curtains** or pillow covers, you may discover that you do just fine. And even though items with "some assembly required" take some time to put together, you don't have to pay someone to do the job for you. You're probably going to get a little dirty and make a few mistakes along the way, but that will make what you accomplish all the more rewarding in the end.

Luckily, there are helpful resources all around you. Home supply stores such as Lowe's and Home Depot give beneficial advice on decorating. These stores are in the business of showing consumers how to choose paint, find the proper tool, or install a tile backsplash or a faucet. They feature workshops on how to do your own home improvements. They'll also help you find a contractor who can do that odd job you don't want to attempt.

Even without leaving your house, you have a wealth of information at your fingertips on the Internet. Just by typing a word or phrase into a search engine like Google or Yahoo, you can immediately access hundreds if not thousands of Web sites devoted to helping you with your home projects.

Understand that room transformation won't happen overnight. Unlike the magic on television decorating shows, the

TOOLS YOU NEED

▶ When you start a decorating project, you want to keep everything together. I'd suggest a tote bag to keep everything in one place for your decorating project. It offers convenient storage that's easy to carry. In the tote bag you should have such things as fabric swatches, carpet squares, tile samples, paint chips, a tape measure, a floor plan of the room you're decorating, and pictures of pieces you'd like to buy.

ELSEWHERE ON THE WEB

▸ The Web sites for home supply stores like Home Depot (www.homedepot .com) and Lowe's (www .lowes.com) are a ready source of information for home decorators. They feature more than what the store is trying to sell, such as useful articles on home projects that detail what supplies and skills you'll need. In addition, they can save you a lot of time tracking down a particular item to order.

before and after stages of decorating don't flow quickly. There are always unexpected events that make a project take longer than it seemed on the drawing board.

However, thorough planning can cut down on the time needed to complete your project. Instead of rushing into it, talk to other people who have completed such a project. Can you learn anything from their experiences? Ask questions of knowledgeable staff at home stores. Factor in the weather when doing projects like painting. The coat of **primer** might take longer to dry before you can apply the paint, and you might need to give a job two or more coats.

And—very important—read directions. One reader reported that the **laminate floor** he was trying to install kept buckling until he read the directions and learned that he was supposed to open the packages of flooring and let them rest for a certain period of time before installation. Rushing into the project nearly ruined all the flooring, he revealed, before he discovered his mistake.

The work will always look worse before it looks better. Few home projects are accomplished without producing a mess. Make sure you get several plastic drop cloths to cover furniture and flooring. If you're like me, you'll want to cover yourself from head to toe to avoid hair and limbs speckled with paint when you return to work on Monday, after a weekend spent painting the living room walls.

Recruit friends and family to help you do pre-project prepping and post-project cleaning up. They can give advice as well as lend some helping hands. You'll have enough to do to complete any sizable project, let alone trying to clean up afterwards all by yourself. And besides, the more the merrier! Home projects can turn into project parties that leave lasting memories.

Get Linked

On my Interior Decorating site on About.com, you will find more information about the subjects addressed in this chapter. The links below provide further assistance.

TIPS FOR QUICK DECORATING CHANGES

Sometimes you spend more time trying to think of how to do something than it actually takes to do it. This page offers a long list of Quick Tips to get you on track.

http://about.com/interiordec/solutions

BEFORE YOU MOVE INTO YOUR NEW HOME

When the moving truck arrives with your belongings is not the time to think about making major changes in the new house. But there are some things that you can do before you move into a new home that will be much easier when the house is empty.

http://about.com/interiordec/beforemove

DECORATE YOUR HOME FOR A QUICK SALE

When you're ready to move from your home, you don't want some irritating detail to keep would-be buyers from making an offer. Here you'll find some good advice about making some simple decorative changes that really pay off.

http://about.com/interiordec/readytosell

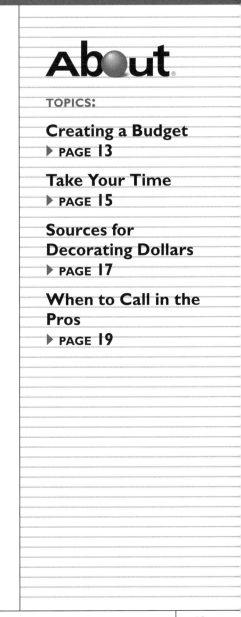

Chapter 2

Decorating Costs

Creating a Budget

Here comes that word so many people don't like: budget. If you tend to shy away from setting an amount to spend on a project, it's time to rethink your resistance to budgeting. When you set up a budget, you decide how much you want to spend on items ahead of time. Decorating your home is an important task, but it's not worth going into debt over. Budgeting both time and money can save you a lot in the long run.

A budget helps you set priorities. For instance, let's say you have a budget of $500 to buy paint and accessories to freshen up your living room. Then you come across some incredible silk pillows that cost $100 each. You know that if you buy three of those pillows, you'll only have $200 left to spend on paint and other things you need for the room. Sure, you can get the pillows and still buy everything else you want by ignoring your budget. But if you spend more than you planned, will that mean you won't have

Prices are through the roof! How can we stretch our dollars?

▶ My experience has shown that paint and other decorating materials go on sale often. Watch ads around holidays, when people fix up their homes for visits by family and friends. The big home improvement stores target Memorial Day and Labor Day as times for homeowners to work on their houses. Sign up for their e-mail newsletters, and you'll be notified of special sales, promotions, and discounts.

money to decorate other rooms? You're suddenly forced to think about what's most important to you.

Great new bath towels and a shower curtain do wonders to brighten up a bathroom, but if the **caulking** around the tub is peeling, that's going to detract from the look. Cracked floor tiles are not only ugly, but they can be a safety issue as well. And while it's more fun to spend the decorating budget on those fancy kitchen cabinet knobs, maybe a new faucet would be a better idea.

A home inspector can help you assess important aspects of your home. You can probably tell if you need new tile in the bathroom, but you may not be such an expert in more structural matters. For instance, it's always a good investment of money to hire an inspector for plumbing or electrical issues. Any problems in these two areas can lead to nasty surprises and expensive service calls, even more extensive work, after you've spent your budget on cosmetic touches.

Home inspectors look at:

- Exterior aspects of the house (such as walls, roof, chimney)
- Heating and air conditioning systems (and estimated life)
- Windows and doors
- Evidence of wood rot or insect infestation
- Water or storm damage
- Plumbing and electrical systems
- Fireplaces (sometimes an additional inspection by a licensed fireplace inspector is recommended)
- Attic and crawl spaces (good ventilation and insulation)
- Floors
- Foundation and basement

Spending a few hundred dollars for an inspection can save thousands of dollars in repairs and renovations later. Just like with other professionals, make sure your inspector is trained and licensed. Check the American Society of Home Inspectors (ASHI) Web site (www.ashi.com) for more information and a list of inspectors in your area. Your real estate agent can probably also give you the name of an inspector you can trust.

Materials and labor can cost more than you might think. Home improvement projects can often turn into much bigger jobs—and cost far more—than originally planned. But then again, what doesn't in life? I find that there are fewer surprises if you take a little time to do some research into prices before you start a project.

Look over newspaper ads, do some research on the Internet, and spend a few hours and a gallon or two of gas visiting some stores in your area. Carry along a notebook to jot down facts and prices so you don't have to rely on your memory. And don't let yourself be pressured to make a decision until you're ready. Ask friends and family to keep an eye out for you on bargains. The more people looking out for what you need, the more likely you'll find what you want for the price you want to pay. And sometimes one of these individuals knows not only of a place that carries the item you need, he knows of someone who can do the work assembling it, installing it, or painting it.

Take Your Time

Sometimes people think that home decorating and renovation have to be done all at once, even if it means putting themselves at risk financially. But why? One room at a time can be a joy to work on, but taking on a whole house all at once can just be painful—both

▶ The idea of "doing it yourself" has really taken off. You can find dozens of books in the bookstore with "DIY" in the title, and there's even a DIY television network (www.diynetwork.com). Whatever the reason for this trend, it's inspiring news for you as you decorate your home. Visit Web sites like www.doityourself.com to find out how you can handle even the trickiest projects at home on your own.

financially and emotionally. It's much smarter to proceed at a pace that works for you.

Here's an anecdote: One of my clients decided she wanted to buy her own home after years of living in a small apartment. Since she didn't make a lot of money, she watched the ads, talked with her realtor, and asked friends and family to watch out for a house she could afford. With house prices rising in her area, her prospects weren't looking good.

And then it happened: She found a house that the bank was **foreclosing** on the property because the homeowner hadn't paid the **mortgage**.

Buying the house was all she could manage, especially since she was forced to act quickly. She used some savings and a small IRA for the down payment, and she knew no decorating binge would be possible. She didn't have much furniture after years in a small apartment, but she had no budget for buying rooms of furniture anyway, especially because the house needed some repairs.

On top of everything, the previous homeowner had taken every light fixture as he walked out the door. (This sort of thing can happen with foreclosures.) Orange shag carpeting covered the floors. Even if she could have handled looking at the color of the rug, it smelled terrible. The owner had let his dog urinate on it, and even professional cleaning wasn't going to get the smell out.

While she waited to close on the house, we worked up a budget for repairs and decorating and planned what projects to tackle first. And my client watched every home improvement show she could find time for. That gave her the confidence to try painting the living room and dining room herself. I suggested she try painting one wall a color she liked and then go on to the other rooms one or two walls at a time on weekends.

Getting rid of the carpet solved one problem, but it presented another: Underneath was concrete. Determined not to get into any more debt, my client found area rugs at secondhand stores and put them on the floor. She didn't have a lot of friends and family over for a while. She worked on her monthly budget a little more, looking for additional places to save. She gave up ordering $3 cups of coffee in the morning, buying an insulated mug and taking her own coffee to work. She packed her lunch every day. Well, almost every day. Once every two weeks or so, she treated herself to lunch out with friends so she could tell them about the progress she was making.

The effort paid off. Little by little my client made her house into a place she could really call home. With enough patience and determination, you can do it too!

Sources for Decorating Dollars

Looking for extra dollars for that decorating project? Sometimes they can be reaped from places you haven't even thought of looking at. What about putting aside 20 percent of each paycheck? Will you receive a tax return? And don't forget good old-fashioned sales and coupons. The savings can really add up if you're creative enough. Here are a few more ideas:

- **Have a garage sale.** Those items that have been gathering dust and taking up valuable space could be turned into cash for your decorating projects.
- **Subscribe to your local newspaper or** *PennySaver.* These publications always include coupons and advertise great deals in your area. You can save hundreds, even thousands, of dollars on a large decorating project this way.
- **Shop discount stores and outlets.** Stores are springing up everywhere that feature discount home furnishings, flooring, accessories, and more. Even if you don't live close to one of these places, it can be worth the drive to check out the prices.

How do I know what my stuff is worth? What will people pay at a garage sale?

▶ Anyone shopping a garage sale is looking for a bargain, so keep that in mind when you price your things. Unless you have a highly collectible or unique piece, you'll make your money by volume sales, not on an individual piece. Think what you'd be willing to pay for the items if you were the one bargain shopping and price them accordingly.

● **Look for deals online.** There are lots of Web sites that offer inexpensive ways to buy almost anything you can think of and have it shipped to you. Just make sure you pay attention to shipping costs.

You can also save by doing projects yourself that you might normally contract out. For example, it's very easy to recover a chair seat. Just turn the chair over and sometimes the seat itself will pop out. If it's the kind that is screwed into the chair, just unscrew the seat. Take off the existing material and use it as a **template** to cut new fabric in the correct size. Simply place this over the seat, turn it over to staple it in place, then reinsert it into the chair. Voilà—a new look for just a few dollars.

Don't throw away those old drapes, either. Dress them up with some fringe, tassels, or trim, or put sheers behind them. Some drapery materials can be dyed by your dry cleaner or put in the washer with dye you can buy at the grocery store. If you're truly fed up with the drapes, consider making them into throw pillows, chair cushions, or even big floor cushions to sit on while you watch television.

Do you have a favorite chair that looks like it has seen better days? If you truly love it and can't envision living without it, then it's worth the cost of reupholstering. If that's out of the budget, try a **slipcover**. Many of the companies that manufacture sofa covers make wonderful covers for chairs as well.

Reupholstering isn't as difficult as it seems. Think about trying it on a chair. One of my favorite tips is to cover only the seat portion of the chair to give it a new look. A mixture of fabrics can add spice to a room and save dollars if you can't find or afford enough fabric to do the whole chair. Remember when you reupholster a chair or sofa to use a fabric that can stand up to wear. Also be careful with fabrics with obvious grain so this doesn't run in all directions when the material is sewn together.

When to Call in the Pros

OK, so you feel you've done all you can to save on labor on your project. And maybe the repairs are such that you aren't trained or licensed to do, such as move walls or perform major electrical or plumbing work. Not only are these tasks dangerous for the untrained, they often require permits.

Those home decorating shows make opening up rooms look so easy, don't they? But trained contractors are doing the work of knocking down those walls, and I can tell you they've made sure they're not going to hit live electrical wires or bring down the ceiling on their heads.

Ask friends who have had home renovations or repairs for the names of reputable contractors and businesses. Then check these out through the Better Business Bureau in your community. Your home insurance agent or realtor may be able to supply you with the names of some good companies.

Here are some tips on how to avoid a rip-off with contracted home repair or renovation:

- Don't hire anyone who shows up at your door to say he's working in your neighborhood and can do the work really cheap.
- Don't use a family member or friend who doesn't have the required skills, even if he'll do it for free.
- Don't try to do the work without a permit if one is required.
- Keep in mind that the low bidder may not be the best person to do the work. Check out his references and look at what he's done.

No matter what, make sure you have a signed, written contract before you have anyone hammer one nail in your home. The

ASK YOUR GUIDE

Money isn't the issue. I just don't have the time to do my own decorating. What should I do?

▶ This is the time to call in another professional—a home decorating professional. She can help you to figure out what you want to do and then take care of all the details for you. You can choose just how much or how little you want to be involved. Remember that it's your house. A decorator should do only what you want within your budget.

contract can be a simple matter of you signing the estimate you've been given and specifying the repairs, the total price, and the date by which they'll be completed. If it's a big project, the contract might be longer or more complicated. Guidelines for home repair including a model contract are available at **www.ago.state.ms.us/divisions/consumer/factsheet**.

Get Linked

At my About.com site on Interior Decorating, I've written more about deciding whether to hire a decorator or a contractor. Check out the following helpful links.

DO YOU NEED TO HIRE A PROFESSIONAL INTERIOR DESIGNER?

I've put together some questions to ask yourself. If you answer yes, you'll need some professional decorating help.
http://about.com/interiordec/hirepro

SHOULD YOU BE THE PROJECT COORDINATOR FOR YOUR HOME DECORATING?

Do you think about decorating all the time? Do you know all the best stores to shop for decorating items? If so, maybe you should manage your home decorating.
http://about.com/interiordec/doityourself

WORK WITH A DECORATOR EVEN IF YOU'RE ON A BUDGET

Not everyone has money to hire a private decorator to make all the arrangements for a home remodeling project. But there are a number of sources for professional help at low cost or no cost.
http://about.com/interiordec/budgetdecorator

Chapter 3

What's Your Style?

Your Decorating Past, Present, and Future

Reflect on the evolution of your decorating style over the years. Chances are it has changed course a number of times, and you might still be wondering what your style actually is. This is the case for many people, especially those who have always had their decorating decisions made for them. Think about it: Your furniture was probably chosen for you as a child. Then as a teen, you might have gotten to make a few decisions about your living space, though not many. Later if you landed in a dorm room, your furniture was likely chosen by the school and limited to whatever would fit into a tiny room. Decorating the bed, often a standard metal one, with a colorful bedspread and hanging a few posters on the wall was probably the extent of your decorating experience. And a first apartment furnished with hand-me-downs from parents and a few items from a secondhand store isn't any more creative a work. Over the years, our living arrangements result in a conglomeration

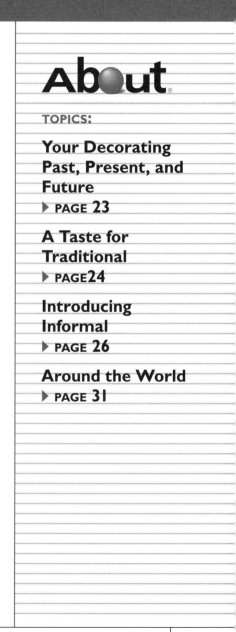

▶ **Trends** exist in decorating just as they do in hairstyles, clothing, music, and so many other aspects of our society. Decorating trends encompass the latest in colors, in furniture styles, in accessories. A trend proclaims what's hot, what's unusual, what's "now." But be careful: What's hot right now is not usually very hot in a few months. Make sure the home décor you choose appeals to you and not just to the trendsetters out there.

of styles and mismatched pieces. Is it any wonder that most of us start our adult life not knowing which style we like best?

Now assess your current home decorating status and what you want to work toward in the future. Are you looking to give your first place some personal flavor and flair without emptying your wallet? Are you a bit older and ready to replace items from your younger days? Or are you firmly settled but tired of the style that you committed to years ago? No matter what your age, decorating history, or current situation, you can achieve your home decorating goals. This doesn't have to be a complicated process dictated by rules. The truth is that though there are plenty of particular styles out there, you don't necessarily have to pick one and stick to it. A home integrated with a few different styles can be very interesting and inviting. What matters is that you feel at home.

A Taste for Traditional

Traditional style has a predictable quality that many people enjoy. Almost everyone feels comfortable with traditional-style rooms. Traditional style feels familiar because it's the most popular decorating style and the one we see most often. Traditional tends to be formal, with antique furniture and accessories, original oil paintings and lithographs, Persian and Oriental rugs, and **chandeliers** and light fixtures of crystal or brass. Windows are tall and have elaborate coverings.

You'll find examples of traditional or formal decorating styles in elegant older homes, historic homes, and some hotels. **Antebellum** homes in the South offer good examples of traditional furnishings and decorating. Even in homes that don't feature traditional decorating throughout the house, you'll often find a traditional dining room because it provides comfort and hospitality for those big holiday dinners.

▲ A traditional-style living room

American traditional is different from European traditional, even though its roots are in Europe. As Europeans migrated to the colonies, they brought their traditions with them but adapted these to a more casual and rigorous lifestyle. Fabrics became more rugged, decoration was downplayed, colors became livelier, and there was less ornamentation. Furniture was practical, less ostentatious, befitting the new American way of life.

Want to introduce a traditional decorating style into your home? Try these easy tips:

ELSEWHERE ON THE WEB

▶ Waverly is a fabric, floor covering, and wallpaper company that offers choices of many interior decorating styles. The Web site has a simple quiz that you can take to help identify your decorating personality. Focusing on your lifestyle, likes, and dislikes, the questions help you zero in on the colors, window treatment styles, and accessories that can make a space feel your own. The quiz can be found at www.waverly.com/Decorate/LIFEQUIZ.asp.

- Add decorative, comfortable pillows.
- Feature a few good furniture pieces in quality woods.
- Choose lush, cozy fabrics.
- Use rich paint colors and decorative painting techniques such as stencils and **faux** painting.
- Consider a chandelier or other elaborate decorative lighting such as a lamp with brass or crystal.
- Arrange furniture in formal groupings such as pairs of chairs, tables, or lamps. Balance these at either end of sofas, picture windows, an **armoire**, or a big piece of art.

Introducing Informal

Does traditional seem a little too structured, too formal for you? The very structure and symmetry that make the style feel familiar to most people can also make it seem less than comfortable for those seeking a more relaxed atmosphere in their home. Traditional style can also limit choice for those who want to experiment with color and fabric. If you prefer a more casual setting, maybe informal is for you. The informal style is homey, warm, and inviting. It's the style people choose when they want above all to be relaxed in their own homes. Informal rooms make use of:

- **Long, large and horizontal furniture pieces.** Tables are chunky and large-scale, which gives an ample feeling while providing space for storage and spreading out.
- **Neutral colors** like tan, gray, beige, and off-white with earth tones.
- **Simple details and soft upholstery.** Accents don't have to be arranged symmetrically.
- **Natural fabrics** such as cotton, linen, and wool. New synthetic weaves give a natural look and add durability.

- **Window coverings** in the form of **shutters,blinds**, or shades as well as simple panels.
- **Found items** of wicker, iron, **rattan**. Flea market finds fit in as well as old antiques.
- **Simple collections,** often family photos grouped on a table or **mantel**.

Flooring in informal decorating tends to be hardwood, tile, stone, or stained concrete. If carpet is used, it shouldn't be too plush. Choose **sisal**, Berber, long, shaggy styles, or subtle geometric, woven patterns.

Informal decorating is easily expressed in various styles. A few of these include rustic, cottage, and shabby chic, each of which is described next.

If you like informal style, you'll love rustic. It's a style that appeals to an independent spirit, someone who enjoys practical comfort and the warmth and colors of nature. While some associate rustic with log cabins and mountains and Western locales, a true lover of rustic can make even a New York loft feel warm and homey.

There's a practicality about rustic décor. Durable fabrics like **denim** are a must. Accent pieces are often practical items found in a country cabin or an outdoor setting, such as spatterware dishes in a kitchen or a weathered wagon wheel used as a chandelier over a dining room table.

Whether you want to go all out or just have a few items that evoke a rustic look, you're choosing an all-American style that will make you, your family, and friends feel rusticated.

For a rustic décor, try some of the following:

- A leather or suede sofa
- Iron or antler candlesticks

- Mirrors framed in hammered **pewter** or tarnished silver
- Hand-loomed plaid or striped blankets or throws, even horse blankets
- Framed prints of deer, moose, horses, birds, or any wildlife associated with your area
- Rough-hewn furniture or furniture made of twigs
- Stone accents around fireplaces

Rustic can be used in all or just one of your rooms to create a warm, cozy, earthy decorating style that can make it hard for you and your family to leave home.

▲ A rustic-style chair

Do you long for a cottage? Want to get away to a cottage by the sea or in the country but have no budget for a second home? You might want to try the cottage decorating style. A beach or lakeside cottage evokes fresh air, the moon over the water, and breezes fluttering the curtains at an open window. Bare floors suit cottage lovers just fine; they appreciate the carefree feel of wood beneath their feet without having to worry about getting sand in the carpet. Blues and greens suggest the sea or a nearby lake and work well with neutral colors like sand. Shells and driftwood found on shore walks serve as natural decoration.

Country cottage lovers favor the serene setting of gardens, fields, and quiet woods. The style celebrates a calm environment and the simple things in life, away from the hustle and bustle of city life.

Since cottage spaces are small and cozy, they can present storage problems. So cottage lovers become crafty and make every object and space count. Wicker trunks and baskets hide blankets and papers, shelves display collections, and quilts and other decorative textiles become art for the wall as well as coverings for the bed and sofa.

Shabby chic is cottage's cousin. It's just what it sounds like— chic style that's a little shabby, in the sense of lived in. Designer Rachel Ashwell coined (and copyrighted) the term to express her casual style that uses vintage accessories, pastels, and cushy furniture. Languidly worn and imperfect furnishings—a look that after all has been around for a long time—suddenly became respected as a decorating style when Ashwell made this chic. Shabby chic is evoked by old lace tablecloths, dreamy and soft floral fabrics, light-painted furniture, wrought-iron curtain rods hung with filmy, sheer curtains, and colorful fresh flowers. It's not so much specific

ELSEWHERE ON THE WEB

▶ The creator of shabby chic, Rachel Ashwell, talks about the development of her decorating style and shows beautifully decorated interiors at www.shabbychic .com. The casual elegance of slipcovered furniture, painted accessories, and soft colors is her hallmark. There you can buy furniture, fabrics, window treatments, books, and accessories that will transform your space into a well-appointed shabby chic interior. Or on your own collect pieces from flea markets, garage sales, and attics. What could be easier?

▶ Want to duplicate that vintage, aged look without paying a high price? Try staining fabrics with tea. You'll need a sink, large bowl, or your washing machine. And tea bags, of course. Make the tea in hot water and submerge your lace or fabric until you get the color you want. Tint the pieces a little darker than desired because the color will be lighter as it dries. And keep in mind that it will fade as it's washed.

pieces as a particular sensibility that balances elegance with old and weathered patinas, shiny silver accessories with painted wooden tables, soft throw rugs with rough old lace.

Shabby chic may well be the easiest and least expensive way to furnish your space with a unique decorating style. Try soft, delicate colors—soft white, muted gray, pale pink and faded green for walls and carpeting. Be creative in combining patterns and colors; use stripes, checks, and floral fabrics to achieve a warm and inviting look. Gather fabrics from yard sales and flea markets. You don't have to follow traditional rules of combining prints but for easiest mixing, keep the background color the same (for example, white or ivory). Then to unify the look, choose one color to repeat in almost every fabric, such as a soft green or pale pink.

You'd be surprised how a coat of paint can transform a dark, dingy chair or table. And think outside the box: Not every chair is for sitting nor do pieces have to be used in tradition-bound ways. Don't be afraid of using a sturdy, painted straight chair as a table beside a bed or sofa or by itself in a corner to hold a vase of flowers. Be creative and use what you have.

Architectural details add interest to the shabby chic look. Anything old and beautiful will work: glass doorknobs, pillars, an old mantle, and rusted old iron brackets or hooks add texture to any room.

Everything old is new again with a casually shabby interior. Even the most broken-down or dingy but elegant formal furniture pieces can be adapted to this décor. If it's broken, fix it, clean it up, and paint it white. If it's rusted, clean it up (but only a little) and find it a new home. Because the look is so adaptable, it's a perfect way to decorate a guest room or family room. With the focus on warmth and lightness, everyone will be charmed.

Around the World

Design influences come from many countries, cultures, and historical periods. After all, as people move they bring with them the things that they love, from food to furnishings. You might feel most comfortable with what your forebears had in their homes. Or maybe you just want a different style. Whether you have family heirlooms or objects from your family's cultural frame of reference, I believe you should fill your home with what you like. There are so many rich design influences. Choose from the global selection that speaks to you.

Hispanic culture has influenced decorative style. In the last few years, the number of Hispanic Americans has grown in the United States, influencing the décor scene. This decorating style is vibrant and warm, with sun-kissed colors, earthiness, and citrus tones. Rich, carved-wood furniture pieces are usually large and important in the room. Metal accents such as tooled leathers, scrolled iron, wrought-iron handles, chandeliers, and architectural items add interesting rustic accents.

One of the people credited for bringing this decorating style to the nation's attention is Spanish language TV talk show host Cristina Saralegui. Interviewers visiting her Miami area home come away praising its sunny colors, richly carved furniture, and terra cotta tiles. Furniture makers have been clamoring for her to design for them and lend her name to Latino-influenced collections.

Do you love the exotic? Wear animal prints and love lush fabrics and colors? Tropical chic might be for you. This doesn't mean making your home look like a jungle with huge palm trees and **murals** of grinning monkeys. Instead, grass cloth wallpaper lends a warm, textured finish as do natural fiber rugs like sisal. Window coverings can be bamboo blinds or wooden shutters. Curtains should stay simple and be made from natural fabrics like linen and cotton.

A number of big-name companies have introduced furniture lines with dark woods like mahogany and teak in addition to stylish rattans, woven bamboo, and other materials from the tropics. Think of Humphrey Bogart in Casablanca and of Ernest Hemingway's beloved Key West. This is a look to carry you away from everyday life.

▲ A tropical-style bedroom

With influences akin to British Colonial, tropical chic can decorate just a room or an entire home. Or just use a few elements like **matchstick blinds** or gauzy sheers, a grass cloth rug covering cool tiles on the floor, and simple furniture pieces upholstered in natural fabrics like linen. Add a few whimsical touches like a pair of candlesticks decorated with monkeys or a ceramic parrot resting on a side table.

French Country has elegant appeal. Sunny yellow and Breton blue are two colors most closely associated with French Country, although reds and other earth tones are also used. French Country is rustic but a little more elegant than other country styles.

If you've visited France and loved the fields of lavender, vineyards, the old farmhouses with their stone floors, mellow colors, and warm, welcoming kitchens, French country may be the decorating style for you. Architectural elements include distressed wood ceiling beams and timbers, stone walls and floors, stone fireplaces, and irregular, painted plaster walls.

As for furniture, a big armoire is a must in the kitchen to store pots and pans and in the bedroom and bath to store clothing and linens. A traditional design for French country fabrics features a white, cream, or yellow ground with large motifs in a single contrasting color, such as black, blue, red, or green. The fabrics are called **toile**, whose themes include farm animals, country scenes, monkeys, Chinese patterns, and courting scenes of the eighteenth century. Most toile patterns are printed on linen or cotton.

Add traditional French country products and motifs such as roosters, olives, sunflowers, grapes, lavender, and beetles. The designs are often arranged in regular intervals, bordered by a wide

ELSEWHERE ON THE WEB

▶ For a look at truly French country interior accessories, fabrics, furniture and art, visit the site for Pierre Deux at http://pierredeux.com. Their products are of the highest quality and can be a bit pricey, but the Web site shows the style at its best. You can use it as a resource for finding items that you need for a French country décor.

panel of the motifs in different scale. Flowers fill baskets, pitchers, pots, and vases.

Tuscan-style decorating has some of the same romantic elements as French country. This includes sun-washed colors and a feeling of being connected to the earth. Terra cotta, brick, ochre, greens, and golden yellow are the pervasive colors. Blues and greens add a visual cooling effect in areas with hot weather. Surfaces that have been painted add a dash of color even when the finish wears off.

Often walls are painted a soft white or gray while accent colors, natural woods, and stone provide interest. Ceilings have dark, open timbers. Venetian plaster is a technique for adding texture and color to new walls.

Open cupboards and armoires are found in almost every room and are used for dishes, linens, and clothes. Door frames are often left open with chicken wire. No Tuscan kitchen is complete without a long, family-style wooden table. Open shelves and free-standing cupboards provide storage in a Tuscan-style kitchen, providing a place to display ceramics and pottery. Kitchen sinks are made of natural stone or porcelain. Cabinet and sink hardware are often of dark wrought iron. Install a copper range hood surrounded by tumbled marble tiles at the stove area and display copper pots hanging from a wrought-iron rack. Use terra cotta containers as accents and storage, and add color with majolica (a type of glazed earthenware) dinnerware.

Eclectic uses a mixture of styles. I think eclectic is one of the most popular styles because of this natural combining of influences. Many people want to be surrounded by objects that they love without conforming to or being limited by a single decorating scheme.

▲ An eclectic bedroom

In an eclectic room you might have a contemporary sofa, an antique secretary, a Chinese screen and, underneath it all, a Persian rug. No one style should predominate. There are, of course, a few prohibitions. For instance, I don't think you can combine elements of a shabby chic room with a contemporary look. But in general you can combine the things you love in your space in such a way that everything works together. And remember, your room decorated in an eclectic style will be a unique combination that no one else will have. By incorporating elements from different backgrounds and cultures, for example, combining the best of European, South American, African, and South Seas styles, interiors can look highly interesting. In such an eclectic setting each individual piece takes on a special meaning and points to an inhabitant's diverse interests, travels, and heritage.

Get Linked

On the About.com site for Interior Decorating, I've included resource information on characteristic decorating styles.

DECORATING STYLE GUIDES

You can read detailed articles about many of the most popular decorating styles, including traditional, formal, informal, French country, and many more.

http://about.com/interiordec/styleguides

STYLE QUIZ

If you're really stuck with determining your personal style, you might want to answer questions about your likes and dislikes in home decorating. Afterward, you should be able to put a name to what style you like.

http://about.com/interiordec/stylequiz

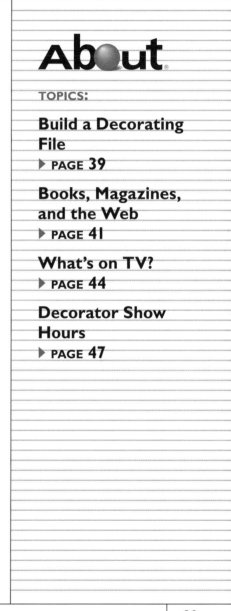

Chapter 4

Looking for Inspiration

Build a Decorating File

It may sound like a cliché, but inspiration is all around us. Decorating ideas can come from nature, from an accessory you see when you're out shopping, or from visiting a friend's house. For this reason, it's important to keep a decorating file of everything you see and hear about as you develop your home decorating plan.

Your decorating file is the place to keep everything you'll be using for your decorating project, from paint swatches to floor plans, carpet samples to fabric cuttings. Be sure to include pictures of your space as it is now and pictures of rooms you're using for inspiration. By having everything in one place, the job will go more smoothly from start to finish.

The notion of a decorating file doesn't mean a file like you'd have in a filing cabinet but a receptacle that will work best for you: a notebook, briefcase, tote bag, or portable file box. Choose a file that you can carry around easily and is big enough for everything you'll have in it.

ELSEWHERE ON THE WEB

▶ Not everyone can be expected to be able to draw an accurate floor plan of their home. If you need more than graph paper and a pencil, check out the Plan 3D site at www.plan3d.com/pages/interiorDesignhome.aspx?rd=1. With the programs they provide (for a fee), you can create on your computer a perfect and accurate drawing of your home.

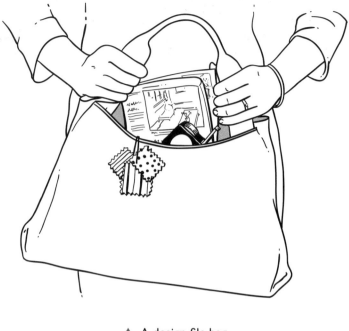

▲ A design file bag

I use a tote bag with shoulder straps and lots of interior pockets. It's a good idea to keep pencils, a tape measure, scissors, and tape in a small container in one of the pockets. Keep a small disposable or digital camera in one of the pockets, too. Organize papers and individual projects in an expanding folder with pockets and labeled divider tabs.

Instead of wondering whether the paint you see will coordinate with a swatch of fabric that you've settled on, you can simply check the paint chips in your decorating file and know right away. With everything together, you'll always be ready.

You'll find the following list of items for your decorating file to be helpful:

- Pencils, pen, and pad of paper
- Tape measure at least twelve feet long
- The floor plan of the room you're working on
- Photos of your room
- Fabric swatches and samples of your flooring
- Paint chips
- Calendar for your work schedule
- Phone list of contractors, workrooms, and stores
- Scissors and tape

Books, Magazines, and the Web

Books and magazines are indispensable in looking for home decorating ideas. Choose a couple of magazines you really like and get subscriptions. That way, you can clip any ideas you like for your decorating file. If you're working with a small budget and don't want to spend lots of money on pricey books and magazine subscriptions, just check out your local library. Although you can't mark up or cut clippings from these resources, you can make photocopies and take notes. And if your local branch doesn't have a particular book or magazine you need, chances are it can order it from another branch nearby.

The Web is also an invaluable resource for design ideas. With the soaring popularity of home design reported in the media, there is no shortage of Web sites and blogs out there for you to peruse. There you can find photo galleries, how-to instructions, tips and tricks, and even order tools and materials and have them delivered to your home.

Books have a lot to offer the aspiring decorator. Many home decorating and design books feature beautiful photography

ASK YOUR GUIDE

Where else can I look for decorating ideas?

▶ If you're looking for an interesting way to spend a Saturday while soaking up ideas for your home, consider visiting museums, auctions, and antique shops. If you're interested in period or antique furniture, you might want to visit the decorative arts departments in area museums. Other possibilities are auction houses, antique stores, and antique shows. Even though you might want to hold off buying anything, finding out about beautiful pieces will increase your appreciation for them and educate you on the value of such items.

that will really get the wheels in your head turning. Whereas magazines might offer you only a taste of a particular style or a short article on how to recreate a look in your home, books often include in-depth instructions, complete with lists of tools you need, materials to buy, and sometimes even patterns and outlines to follow. Big hardcover books with lots of photography can be expensive, so if you can't afford to buy them, check them out of your local library and make photocopies. Many libraries have both black-and-white and color copiers that members can use.

Design magazines feature articles on the latest color and style trends. They're especially helpful for seasonal and holiday decorating ideas. Once you've determined your decorating style, you'll know which magazines to subscribe to or pick up from the newsstand to clip ideas from. In many cases you won't be able to duplicate exactly what you see in the glossy pages of these magazines; however, you can still get lots of inspiration and direction. Not a fan of contemporary? Then maybe *Country Home* is more to your taste.

Here's a list of my favorite decorating magazines and what they feature:

- *Architectural Digest:* This publication showcases homes of the rich and famous. It's a great resource for professional designers, serious homeowners, and those who want to see how the other half lives. It shows state-of-the-art design and gives the average reader professional ideas at a low cost.
- *Verandah:* This magazine features interiors from the southern United States. The sumptuous décors are mostly formal and elegant, and many of the techniques and ideas shown can be incorporated into traditional homes.

- *Traditional Home:* As the title suggests, the focus of this magazine is historic homes and traditional décor. It offers ways to bring traditional styles and resources into today's lived-in interiors. It is a particularly good resource for ideas on pleasing color schemes, information on furniture styles, and classic window treatments.
- *Romantic Homes:* This is a wonderful magazine for the romantic at heart. The pages are filled with pictures of homes decorated in cottage style or shabby chic style. Flowers and ruffles are everywhere. They have a good directory of shopping sources of items for romantic homes.
- *Country Living:* This is a treat for lovers of country-style crafts, antiques, décor, and traditional cooking. Articles and photographs highlight rooms with warm colors, welcoming fireplaces, homey furniture, and basic window treatments.
- *Metropolitan Home:* The magazine features current trends in contemporary style and offers articles on transforming classic traditional space into state-of-the-art urban spaces. Gardening tips for small outdoor spaces are available for readers downsizing into condominiums or apartments.
- *Elle Décor:* Here you'll find sophisticated modern spaces with a French influence. The magazine shows what's hot in luxury living, furniture design, and space planning and offers related resources.
- *House Beautiful:* This is one of the oldest print resources for interior decorating. The magazine offers photos of both classic and up-to-date décor with ideas for kitchens, baths, and living spaces in real homes. You'll also find tips for home remodeling and renovations as well as resources for products.

▶ It's great fun to decorate a room around a theme or special interest. The design reality TV shows are experts at tying everything together in a room, usually based on a color scheme or theme. Whether a fairy tale, favorite sport, travel destination, or special interest, a cohesive theme helps to give purpose and direction to decorating a room. Choose a theme, then think of everything you already own that lends itself to that theme. Costumes, hats, maps, sporting goods— nothing is off limits.

- *Country Home:* This magazine offers articles on antiques and collectibles, craft projects and country decorating ideas. Charming country gardens are featured and recipes for good home-style food are included.
- *Better Homes & Gardens:* This is another long-time favorite in traditional homes. Although there's nothing cutting edge here, the magazine offers ideas for home décor, gardening, and family activities. It caters to the average homeowner or renter and provides practical solutions to common challenges. This is a good pick for seasonal projects.

The Internet is an incredible home decorating resource. There are numerous sites devoted exclusively to this subject and countless others that relate in some way. The information on About.com alone can get you where you want to go! Articles are posted or updated almost daily, and simply by clicking a link you can access hundreds of articles—even informative videos and slide shows—on any home decorating topic in the database. Exploring the Web site is just like turning the pages of magazines on home decorating. There are do-it-yourself projects that will make your own decorating project simpler and, I hope, problem free.

What's on TV?

It's no surprise that television is one of the ways we can get decorating inspiration, conveniently sitting right in the middle of our living rooms. And with cable, we have so many different channels to choose from. There were home decorating shows before Home and Garden Television (HGTV) came along but they were few and far between and tended to be repetitive.

Many people have told me they found the courage to do something about a room they'd always wanted to redecorate from watching decorating shows on television. The step-by-step nature of a room being prepped, painted, furnished, and decorated, often on limited budgets (such as on *Decorating Cents* or *Design on a Dime*) made them think they could do the same without using a decorator.

Some of my readers live in small towns and aren't always able to travel to a bigger city to look at furnishings and objects they need to decorate their homes. From television shows they gain access to new products on the market and learn where to buy them. Sometimes readers would like to make decorating changes but they find it hard to get their partners to agree on what those changes should be. *Designing for the Sexes* is valuable for showing couples how to compromise differing tastes (as well as comfort levels with change) to come up with a room both can love.

Today you can get inspiration to clean up and clear rooms from TV shows like HGTV's *Mission Organization* or TLC's *Clean Sweep*. At a minimum, the programs can help you feel better about your own place to the extent that it's less full of stuff than those televised. Watch carefully to discover how homeowners learn to distance themselves from excess things. The shows are helpful as well for seeing the latest in home organization products.

What can you get from home decorating TV shows? Well, besides the entertainment factor, these shows encourage you to be a little adventurous with your decorating. Maybe you've been too conservative in the past. Why not watch an episode of the show and see if you don't get an inspiration to break out of that safe rut?

Perhaps the show with the highest drama quotient is *Extreme Makeover: Home Edition*. Talk about extreme! A huge crew of demolition, landscaping, building, finishing, and decorating experts do in one week what even the luckiest homeowner would need four months to do. The show debuted in late 2003 on ABC and chooses families based on extreme need, community involvement, and audience appeal.

You can draw inspiration from the show for your own home decorating by, for example, choosing a theme to decorate your child's room and thinking of every way you can incorporate the theme into the décor. Or you might decide that the best way to change a room is to get rid of everything in it. Then bring back only what you really want. Be ruthless and stick to your guns. When you're done, you'll be able to see what you need to complete the project.

The show *Trading Spaces* on TLC recruits neighbors to help decorate their friends' house. Keys are exchanged, blinds and draperies are drawn, and the transformations begin. A crew of designers and carpenters has just two days to redecorate the room before time is up. One thing's for sure—there are lots of surprises. Is a neighbor who would cover your bathroom walls with moss (for a natural look) really your friend?

Some of the shows reveal just how easy and inexpensive it is to transform the look of a room with paint. You've seen different paint treatments done in magazines. But you might not believe that it's easy to paint stripes, squares, or borders until you see someone actually demonstrate the techniques using blue painter's tape to mark off the areas.

Program hosts show how to stain furniture or use scraps of material to change the fabric on the seats of a dining room chair. You'll see them make simple **Roman shades** with new products like a cloth tape. All of these demonstrations can inspire you to try a simple project that takes a small amount of time, help you gain confidence with a job well done, and move you on to bigger and more complicated tasks, some that take more money as well.

▶ A favorite thing to make on many home decorating shows is a padded headboard for a bed. This project is actually easier than you might think. You'll need a large piece of plywood, tape measure, butcher paper, upholstery foam, batting, lining fabric, outer fabric, a jigsaw, staple gun, cording or trim, and nuts and bolts. Most of the items can be found at a fabric store and home improvement center. You can find a helpful tutorial on my Web site at http://about.com/interiordec/headboard.

All of the shows on television today have Web sites for viewers to access. These contain information on new products, store locations, and phone numbers, even detailed instructions on how to clean, paint, furnish, or renovate a room or an entire house. Download photos and printed information and tuck it into your decorating file so that you can access it when you work on your home. Television decorating shows can be a wealth of information, a very up-to-the-minute resource as valuable as decorating magazines and books.

Decorator Show Houses

Decorator show houses are a worthy venue for people who love design and also love a good cause. They're organized to bring together fundraisers, local interior designers, architects, and landscape designers, all of whom transform a home into a feast for the eyes. Designer show houses are often historic structures, some of which are returned to their original condition after years of disrepair and neglect.

Months ahead of the planned show house event, a group of fundraisers and ASID designers form a committee to choose a house from applicants. Then they select a color scheme and theme for the home. Traditionally, designers are selected to decorate one room or outdoor area following the guidelines set forth.

After a total transformation, the public is invited in to tour the home, speak with the designers, and gather design ideas and inspiration. The event benefits everyone. Proceeds from ticket sales generally are earmarked for a local charity. Local designers, merchants, and tradespeople are given publicity and exposure. And the public has the opportunity to meet design professionals in the settings they have designed, see the work of local craftsmen, as well as view furniture, art, antiques, and accessories.

ASK YOUR GUIDE

How can I find a show house in my area?

▶ To find a show house in your area, check out this link on my About.com site: http://about.com/interiordec/showhouselist. Although I update this list regularly, be sure to call the show house ahead of time to confirm hours of operation. Or try contacting the home and garden editor of your local newspaper, a local ASID chapter, or a local interior design firm for locations and dates.

▶ Looking for inspiration right in your own town? Check out some model homes. Unlike a show house, which isn't for sale and is usually a refurbished older home, a model home is one that a builder features in a new housing development. Professional interior designers are hired to make model homes look lived in. You'll find good ideas for ways to tie rooms together in a home for a cohesive look. Don't forget your camera so you can take photos of elements you like.

Some of these events, such as the Pasadena Showcase House of Design, have Web sites with background information on the home, designer listings, ticket information, and driving directions. Some of them are institutions, such as the famous Kips Bay Boys and Girls Club Show House. But whether they are large or small, famous or only known locally, area show houses attract scores of people.

Try attending a show house to gather ideas for your home and to show your support for the local charity and for local artists. Consider volunteering with your local show house to benefit yourself, your community, and local design professionals. You'll be involved in a wonderful community activity, meet interesting people, and get novel ideas for decorating your own home.

While most show houses are open in April, May, and June, a few events are held in February in Florida or in summer and fall in the northern United States. Because many of these show houses are very popular, tickets should be ordered well in advance. Be sure to call ahead to confirm dates, hours of operation, home locations, special events, ticket prices, and parking restrictions or shuttle information.

Here's a list of my choices for the top designer show houses in the United States:

● **Pasadena Showcase House of Design:** Years of work have taught organizers how to run a show house well and provide helpful information to the public. They have raised over $15 million to benefit the Los Angeles Philharmonic Orchestra, schools, and other local nonprofit organizations. Over fifty interior and landscape designers come together in the spring to transform the interior and grounds of a large, elegant home in southern California.

- **Kips Bay Decorator Show House:** For over thirty years this show house in New York has been raising money for the Kips Bay Boys' and Girls' Club programs, becoming the benchmark by which all other decorator showcase houses are judged. New York interior designers donate their time and talents to create unique interior spaces.
- **National Symphony Orchestra Decorators' Show House:** The Women's Committee of the National Symphony Orchestra sponsors this show house to raise money in support of the orchestra's education, outreach, and artistic programs.
- **Lake Forest Showcase House and Gardens:** Chicago's Infant Welfare Society sponsors this showcase in Lake Forest, Illinois every other year in the spring. Proceeds benefit the programs of the organization.
- **The Atlanta Symphony Associates Decorators' Show House & Gardens:** The Atlanta Symphony Orchestra sponsors this event. Over 2,000 volunteers give their time to staff the house, which attracts over 15,000 visitors from mid-April to early May.
- **Minneapolis ASID Designers' Showcase Home:** The Junior League of Minneapolis and the Junior League of St. Paul combine their efforts to sponsor this event in mid-May each year. Proceeds have helped to fund programs supported by these volunteer organizations.
- **Wisconsin Show House:** The goal of this show house is to raise funds to support breast and prostate cancer research at the Medical College of Wisconsin. Held in June in houses along Lake Michigan, this popular event attracts many of the best designers and landscape architects in the Midwest.

- **Marin Designers Showcase:** This showcase, which provides funding for nonprofit organizations in the San Francisco area, has been running for over thirty-five years. It is open from late September to mid-October. A preview party, daily fashion shows, and Thursday Meet the Designer nights are just some of the attractions.
- **The San Diego Historical Showcase House:** This has been the main fundraising effort of the San Diego Historical Society since 1974. From late April through May each year, locals and vacationers can visit the house and enjoy other attractions in the San Diego area.

Even if none of these show house events is in your area, you might find it worthwhile—and a lot of fun—to make a little vacation out of a visit. You'll get to visit another area of the country as well as get special ideas for your home decorating projects.

Get Linked

Finding ideas for new and interesting decorating is one of my passions. I've included some articles about where to look for quality designer touches on the About.com Web site.

DECORATING 101: WHERE TO FIND IDEAS FOR DECORATING

This article has suggestions for getting help and ideas for decorating your new space.
http://about.com/interiordec/findideas

OUR FAVORITE TV DECORATING SHOWS

With the interest in home decorating on the rise, television is a natural vehicle for bringing ideas and techniques to the public. I've listed my favorite in this article.
http://about.com/interiordec/tvshows

SLIDE SHOWS OF DESIGNER SHOW HOUSES

Not everyone can visit a decorator show house. You might enjoy looking at slide shows from recent show houses in the United States.
http://about.com/interiordec/slideshows

Chapter 5

Working with What You've Got

Keep It or Dump It?

Let's face it: Most of us cannot afford to sweep out all our old furnishings and replace them with new furniture, linens, decorations, dishes, and everything else. Besides, who would want to? Many people grow attached to certain belongings for sentimental reasons: Perhaps a close friend brought you that painting from Argentina, or a relative made that chair by hand. Even if such an item is not exactly your taste, you probably like it for the memories and thoughts it brings to mind. There's no need to get rid of these special things, even if they don't seem to fit into your space. After all, if you move out all your personal items and replace them with store-bought pieces, your house could end up looking like a showroom or catalog spread instead of a home.

On the other hand, if you're hanging onto items only because they were gifts from important people in your life, ask yourself

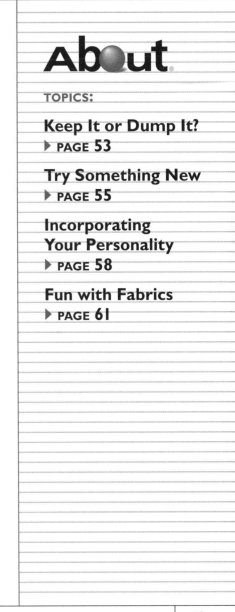

whether this is truly necessary. Chances are those people wouldn't want you to keep an unneeded gift forever. It's completely within your rights to redecorate from time to time, and if you're not attached to an item, you're not obligated to keep it on display. Sell it, give it away, or put it in storage. It's likely Aunt Linda won't notice or remember anyway.

If you're on the fence about keeping or getting rid of an item, do a little experiment. Move the item out of the room for several days and see whether you miss it. If you were always tripping over that stool with the embroidered top and like your room better without it, find a new spot for it or get rid of it. Reclaiming your space and refreshing your surroundings will make you feel empowered and ready for the next step.

There are various means of getting rid of unwanted items. If you have items that are still valuable, you can try to sell them. There are a number of ways to do this:

- **Have a garage sale.** This will allow you to spend some time outside, get to know your neighbors, and make some extra money without even leaving home.
- **Sell items to a local secondhand or antique store.** You might be surprised to learn that your items are more valuable than you thought.
- **Sell items online.** You can post an item and field offers right from your home, and then just mail the items to the chosen buyer. If the buyer is local, you might be able to arrange for pickup at your home. Amazon.com, Craigslist.org, and Ebay.com are great options.

If the items you're trying to get rid of aren't that valuable, or if you don't care about getting money for them, you can choose to give them away. Here are some ideas:

- Offer unwanted items to friends, relatives, and coworkers.
- Post items for free online. Try Craigslist.org or Freecycle .org.
- Give items to a local charity resale shop. Many of these shops choose particular causes to support.

If you're unable to sell or give away an unwanted item, put it out a little early for the trash collection with a sign that says "Free to a good home." A passerby might decide to snatch it up and give it new use, and you'll have newfound space for things you really like.

If you just can't part with an item, put it in storage for a while. If you truly can't bear to get rid of something but you're just tired of looking at it, put it in the attic or basement. After you've had a break you can pull it out again and display it in a new spot. If you don't have much storage space in your home, see if someone else you know will store an item for you. If that's not an option, consider renting a storage unit by the month or the year. You might feel that it's worth the money to rent the space until you either decide you have a place to keep the item or you can finally part with it once and for all.

Try Something New

So, you're not necessarily tired of all your furniture and decorations; you're just tired of where they are and how they're arranged. You just want a refreshing change. No problem! Just because an item has a traditional use (for example, a coffee table sits in front

ASK YOUR GUIDE

I inherited a baby grand piano but never play it and don't have room for it. Any suggestions?

▶ I was in a similar situation. I was given a beautiful upright piano by a very special aunt and uncle. I loaned it to a dear friend. She was thrilled. She put it in a place of importance in her living room and uses it almost every day. At my house, it just took up a wall. I can get it back whenever I need it.

of the couch, a bookcase holds books, etc.) doesn't mean you can't give it a different one. Be creative and think outside the box. A few unlikely items in a room can give your space a unique, intriguing feel. And you can bet these items will make great conversation pieces when you have company.

▲ Blanket basket used as a coffee table,
and a stack of books as an end table

Chances are you already have some items you can use in this way. Go check out the garage, the yard, or the attic. An old cobbler's bench can become a coffee table or end table in a country-style living room or family room. A big pottery planter topped with a piece of glass can also make a great table. **Ottomans** are also making a comeback, often as coffee tables. Just put a tray on top for a stable surface.

For an end table for a rustic room, try an old whiskey barrel like those seen in bars or old country stores or even used as a rain barrel in the old days. If you have a bar area, try putting a fake bottom in a barrel about a foot from the top rim, fill it with corks from wine bottles, put glass atop that and group chairs around it for a place to sit while you enjoy a glass of wine or soda.

▲ An old barrel used as an outdoor dining table

Interested in a garden theme? Try bringing in a little gardening bench as a window seat in a bedroom or the kitchen. Scrub an old birdbath, fill it with **memorabilia** or sand and shells, and top with glass for a clever end table.

Need a place to store your books but can't stand the look of that bookcase in the corner anymore? Stack the bookcase on top of a dresser for a hutch look. I've seen people make frames of wood, fill them with fabric or chicken wire, and use them to close up the hutch for a unique decorator touch. Old bookcases can be used as a divider to separate a too-big room. One clever home-owner picked up a collection of old books with lovely bindings from a used bookstore. He stacked them, drilled a hole through the middle, and inserted the necessary equipment for a lamp. It made a wonderful light source for his den. Just don't use books you'll want to read again!

Incorporating Your Personality

It's obvious that your home wouldn't be your home if it didn't reflect some of your personality, tastes, and interests. Very few people like the look of a sterile showroom for their home. Most people want to feel comforted and cozy in a space that is decorated with things they love. This is where collections and hobbies come into your decorating plan. Using items you already own—and love—is a great way to save money and add personal flair to your space.

Are you a collector? If you keep collections you may already have a lot of what you need for your home decorating projects. No matter what you collect, you can probably find a way to use the items for decoration. For example, say you collect antique cameras. You can group these on a tabletop, coffee table, or shelf for an interesting display. Remember to use a grouping of at least three, and don't scatter the collection around the room—that will only diminish the impact. If you have a large collection, you don't have to put everything out. Instead, think about bringing out a number of pieces and periodically circulate them. That way, you'll always have something new to look at.

Hobbies and passions also make striking decorating themes. For instance, automobiles are a common passion for lots of people. Although I'm not suggesting that you do what some wealthy collectors have done and bring those vehicles inside your home, I have seen some very clever decorating done with automobile parts. Things like metal wheels and other parts can serve as architectural interest on walls in a contemporary room, or you can go all out and make a coffee table of wood supported by a car jack. I once saw an antique motorcycle painted scarlet red with chrome accents, which the owner mounted on a piece of black wood like a sculpture in the corner of his loft living room.

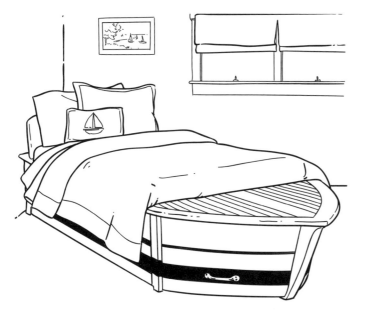

▲ A bedroom with a sailor theme

If you have a hobby such as surfing, why not use something like a surfboard for a coffee table if it suits your decorating style? Yes, a surfboard. There really is no limit to what you can do if you're creative enough. And if you try it and don't like it, the surfboard can go back out in the garage. No harm done.

Have a lot of different interests? Use a combination theme! Not everyone is utterly devoted to one specific sport, hobby, or pastime. Perhaps you dabble in art, music, and the outdoors. There's no reason your home décor can't reflect that mix—even within the same room. Who says you can't have abstract paintings, musical instruments, and bamboo blinds all working in harmony together? You may have to get creative to get it right, but that's what home decorating is all about!

If you're afraid that your tastes will clash or be too overwhelming when combined, use some decorator's tricks to tone things down. Say you want to display a lot of colorful artwork that you picked up on your travels. In this case, a nice neutral paint color for the walls would set them off better than patterned wallpaper. If your curtains display a theme (a floral print, for example), you probably want to stay away from a busy pattern in your furniture upholstery. Some colors or items simply won't look great together no matter what you do, but it's pretty much always worth trying it out to see for yourself.

Giving each theme its own area of a room is a great way of keeping looks from clashing. Try hanging your watercolors of sailboats on the wall with the window that looks out onto the lake, and put your rare book collection on some shelving next to the cozy armchair and reading lamp in the corner. Before long you'll find that you have favorite spots and not just favorite rooms. This will make your home a much more interesting place—for you and your guests.

Fun with Fabrics

If there's one endless source of home decorating potential, it's fabrics. Look around your home. You probably see fabrics everywhere—from the curtains to that blanket folded up on the back of the couch. While you will probably get tired of looking at certain fabrics in your home over time, that doesn't mean they have to go out with the trash. There are countless ways to reuse fabrics in a way that will help you see them in a new light.

Recovering furniture is a great way to give the fabric and furniture new life. Say your design plan means you need new drapes in your living room, but the ones you have are still in very good condition and you still like the fabric. Instead of giving them away, why not find a new use for them? Try recovering a chair or making a slipcover for a **loveseat**.

Do you want to buy your child a new comforter, but he's hesitant to part with the old one? If it's a somewhat durable material, try making it into a beanbag chair cover. You don't even have to go out and buy beans; just look in a consignment or secondhand store for a beanbag that's seen better days and recover it with that comforter.

To spice things up, use fabrics you already have in a new way. For example, you can also use large pieces of fabric to make smaller items. If you want a way to reuse the curtains from your bedroom, why not cut them down and make fabric napkins or placemats? If you have any absorbent fabrics lying around, you can make dish towels for the kitchen. Thick, durable fabrics can be made into lovely potholders. There are so many ways to give the fabrics you love new life!

▲ Use fabric from old curtains or sheets to make pillowcases.

Favorite fabrics also make good decorations. Say you have a beautiful lace napkin that used to belong to your great-grand-mother, but you're not sure how to display it. Have it pressed, mount it in a beautiful frame, and hang it up wherever you like. That way, the napkin will be out where everyone can enjoy it rather than tucked away in a drawer somewhere.

Get Linked

On the Interior Decorating site on About.com there is more information about cleaning out and organizing your home. There are articles and Web links that are quite helpful.

FIND STORAGE SPACE IN YOUR LIVING SPACE

Do you have enough space to store everything you have? Highly unlikely. Find some ways to store items in plain view.
http://about.com/interiordec/storagespace

ORGANIZE YOUR HOME WITH RESOURCES FROM ABOUT.COM

This helpful directory offers many ways to organize your life, from rooms to appointments, to closets and garages.
http://about.com/interiordec/organizelinks

TOP SOURCES FOR FURNITURE BARGAINS

Get some good ideas for finding furniture and household bargains. You might not have thought of them all.
http://about.com/interiordec/furniturebargains

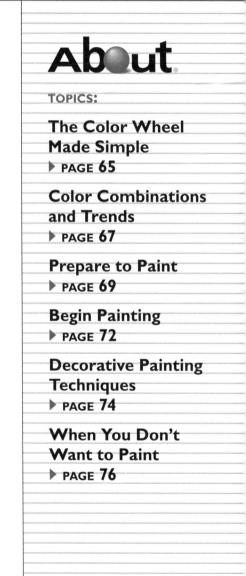

Chapter 6

Start with Color

The Color Wheel Made Simple

Many people live with white walls because they don't feel like they can pick color. And if it isn't hard enough to choose color, paint companies add more colors every year, making the process even more intimidating. Add to this the dwindling amount of time left in the day after work and family concerns, and no wonder why you're living with white walls.

No one wants to spend a lot of time to choose a color, get the supplies, carve out a few hours to paint and put up new curtains, then decide he dislikes the colors he's chosen. But it doesn't have to be that way. It's possible to choose colors in a quicker, easier way and be happy with your choices. I promise! A little study of color principles will go a long way to smooth your path when choosing the right color for your room.

You might remember learning that there are three primary colors: red, blue, and yellow. Other colors are made by mixing two or more of these together. A mixture of two primary colors is called a secondary color. For example, if you mix blue and red you get purple. If you mix blue and yellow you get green. Red and yellow create orange. Red and yellow are considered warm colors and blue and green are cool colors. If you alternate secondary colors with primary colors in a circle, you create a color wheel. Sir Isaac Newton was the first to make a circular diagram of colors in 1666 that has worked well for designers and nonprofessionals alike since then.

Any two colors that are opposite each other on the color wheel are called complementary. By putting two complementary colors—like red and green—near each other, you will create a lot of contrast.

A good way to approach decorating with color is to think about places you love. In fact, rather than working with paint chips and fabric swatches, interior designers often start out by encouraging clients to think of a place that they love. Their memories from that place guide designers to create a room to suit their clients.

Perhaps you love Spain. Think about what colors remind you of that country. Perhaps these are the warm, rich earth tones of greens, browns, and rusts of the region, the beautiful carved woods, and the ironwork found in rustic chandeliers and trim on furniture. Pick your primary color for walls, and then look to the opposite side of the color wheel for inspiration for secondary colors of furniture and floors. Maybe you'll try a burnt orange for an accent wall for your dining room and paint or stain that light-colored furniture that's looking tired. Add simple rustic cloth placemats on the table, a couple of iron candlesticks, and landscapes of the Spanish countryside, and you've changed the whole feel of the room with just a little paint and money.

Color Combinations and Trends

Just like with furnishings and fashion, there are color combinations that seize the imagination of trendsetters. Simply painting a wall or a room with these color schemes will instantly transform a space without your having to go through the trouble and expense of buying new furniture. Here's a list of some of the latest color combinations and trends:

- **Pink and Chocolate Brown:** These are two colors that have been hot on the fashion runways for several years and are still popular. Pink can come in shades of the palest tones of a baby's nursery to shocking fuchsia, depending on how much white, red, blue, or orange is added. Brown adds sophistication to pink.
- **Tan and Black:** These two colors can be dynamite when they are paired. Neutral tans (anything from barely-there taupe to deep golden beige) are a perfect background for trendy black furnishings. By adding white or cream trim and accents of ivory, shiny silver, or gold, the look goes from dark and sophisticated to light and bright.
- **Wild Brights:** There's nothing like a shot of summer color to punch up an interior. Think fresh plums, tangy lime green, Hawaiian punch pink, and turquoise shades of ocean blue. It feels natural to use these colors if you live in a tropical climate. And if you don't, they'll really liven up a room.
- **Pale Blue and a Neutral:** On the other end of the color spectrum, blue and white create a cool, soothing mood in any room. Add cream, brown, black, yellow, or green for accent and brighten up with shiny silver, matte nickel, or colored glass. This classic color scheme always looks fresh and clean.

ELSEWHERE ON THE WEB

▶ Follow True Value Hardware's "Three steps to finding the color that's right for you" to make choosing color simple. According to their Web site, what emotion the color evokes in you is extremely important. The site offers advice from experts, Peel 'n Place paint chips, and four ounce sample bottles to help with decisions. You can also upload your own photos at www .truevaluepaint.com to preview colors before you paint.

▶ Go to HGTV.com and type color personality in the search bar. You'll have fun spinning the color wheel to find out what color personality you are. Like yellow? That's because you're sunny, hopeful, bright, and spontaneous. A green lover? It's because you're natural, healing, refreshing, and you like to solve problems with a fresh perspective, according to the site. That ancient saying, "Know yourself," is never truer than with color choice. Surround yourself with the colors you love and you'll feel revitalized.

- **Soft Gold and White:** Golden **hues** are popping up everywhere and adding a glow to bathrooms, kitchens, living rooms, and bedrooms. This warm color in a range from sunny yellow to golden sunset, accented with white, cheers up any space. Add elegance with aged bronze, dark wood, or black accents.
- **Golden Yellow and Red:** Does your home need some warmth? I prescribe some golden yellow and red to give it some life. Start out with the sunshine of golden yellow walls, add white trim for freshness and clarity, and finish off with tones of red, cranberry, and plum in throw rugs, plaid or patterned fabrics, and accessories.
- **A Soft Neutral and a Pastel:** Who said compromise is difficult? Not with this color scheme. She gets the pastel of her choice with butter yellow, soft turquoise, peach, or delicate green. Add his choice of a warm camel, deep tan, or soft grey. It's smashing and sophisticated, delicate yet definite.
- **Any Tone-on-Tone:** This look is so in fashion right now and so easy to do. Use matte and satin paint together to create tone-on-tone wall stripes. Textured wall coverings create a background that's soothing and sophisticated. Resist the temptation to add other colors unless you want to break the mood. Select a woven or patterned fabric with your chosen color.

Now, if none of these combinations is really your style, that's fine; you have the freedom to experiment with your space. I do recommend, however, that you try out a color by purchasing a small quantity of paint before spending significant money on a combination you're not sure will work out. The virtue of paint is that walls and objects can always be repainted, but unfortunately you can't return custom paint colors to the store once they've been mixed.

Prepare to Paint

I always tell my clients that preparation is the most important step in painting success. And by preparation, I mean everything from getting the right tools, paints, and materials to preparing the walls to be painted. If you don't have the right kind of paint or paintbrush you need, the paint job may not come out the way you'd hoped. And if you don't properly prepare the walls, such as filling in holes and plastering, the paint may not go on smoothly or be as durable as you'd like.

Spend a little time in the paint department looking at paint types, not just colors. There are five main types of paint finishes to choose from. These are:

- **Matte or Flat:** Especially good to hide any imperfections in the wall. This is recommended for older homes.
- **Eggshell:** Picture the low sheen of an eggshell to envision eggshell paint finish. Eggshell holds up better to cleaning than does a flat finish paint.
- **Satin:** Satin finish paint has a smoother look with a bit of gloss. It is most often used for windows, doors, trim, and ceilings but can also be used as wall paint. This finish is recommended for kids' room walls, kitchens, and bathrooms. Satin finishes are formulated to withstand light scrubbing.
- **Semi-Gloss:** Semi-gloss paint is most often used on doors, trim, cabinets, and in kitchens and bathrooms. It cleans up easily but take heed: Poorly prepared surfaces are highlighted by a semi-gloss finish.
- **Glossy:** High-gloss paints have an almost reflective quality, their shiny finish mimicking the look of enamel or plastic. It is not widely used in home interiors, though it is becoming more popular for a dramatic look on cabinets, trim, and

▶ It used to be that all walls and ceilings were painted with flat finish paint and window trim and doors were done in satin enamel. But that was then; this is now. Gloss finishes are spectacular on trim or even a ceiling. How about shiny, glossy walls? Really, you can do anything you want. The rules are out the window, and you can choose a smooth or non-traditional texture for any surface.

furniture in formal and contemporary designs. Again, any imperfections are magnified with this finish.

Choosing eggshell over flat or satin paint, say, depends on the room that's being painted and the effect desired. If you've never chosen paint before, now is the time to discover your own likes. There is no rule you have to follow. Ask questions of your paint consultant at the store, and most of all enjoy the process.

Using a fabric swatch or color chip from your decorating file, choose your paint color and finish. Remember that if you don't find exactly the color you want on the shelf, you can ask the paint consultant to match and mix a custom color using special store equipment. It's amazing what technology can do to produce the perfect color for you.

There are a number of items you need from the store for your paint job. Your shopping list should look like this: paint roller or brush for the type of paint you'll be using (check with your salesperson); a paint stick for stirring; spackle or hole filler; sandpaper or a fine grit sanding block; paint pans and buckets; a flat razor blade to clean up drips; several rolls of painter tape; paint thinner for oil-based cleanup; a drop cloth; and rags for cleanup.

You also need to prepare the room you're planning to paint. Here's a list of chores to do:

- **Clean the walls.** Use a soft brush to clean off any dust, dirt, or paint particles. A clean broom will help you reach high spots. Then clean the walls with a sponge and a mixture of water and a mild detergent. Be sure to let the walls dry completely before proceeding.

- **Patch holes and cracks.** New filler products not only fill holes quickly and easily, they also smooth without needing a lot of the sanding that spackle products used to require. Ask the paint consultant which product is best for your particular wall surface and paint covering. When dry, use a fine grade sandpaper to get rid of excess product and blend in the filled spot with the rest of the wall.
- **Remove all hardware in the room.** Go around the room and remove the electrical cover plates used on switches and outlets. Most can be removed with a **Phillips head screwdriver.** You may want to remove window sash locks and handles. Door knobs and strike plates on the door latch also need to come off. Remove window shades and blinds so they don't get spattered with paint.
- **Create a splatter-proof environment.** The floor or carpet should be protected. You can buy canvas or plastic drop cloths at the hardware or discount store for just a few dollars, which is money well spent. Afterward you'll be glad you took the time to cover everything, no matter how neat you think you'll be in advance. Finally, put those drop cloths over your furniture and anything else you want to protect.
- **Tape and cut in for a professional job.** Take a hint from the professionals and use blue painter's tape to create a clean painting line at ceiling and baseboard and around windows and doors. Be sure to buy the tape specifically labeled for painting, which is created to stick during the painting process but lift off easily without disturbing new paint. Trust me—it's not worth saving money on a cheap substitute.

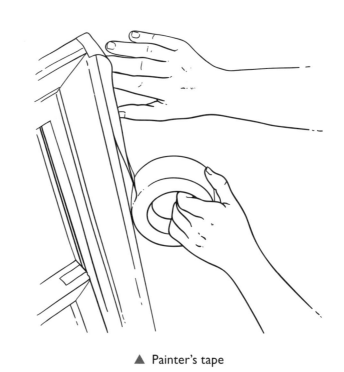

▲ Painter's tape

Once you have gathered your supplies and prepared your room, you're finally ready to begin painting.

Begin Painting

You've picked the paint, cleaned the walls, patched holes, and taped. Now it's time to open up that can of paint you've chosen, right? Well, not yet. I know it's tempting to just rush in and start, but this is a case in which doing a hasty job will lead to repainting more quickly than you'd like. Taking a little more time to do the job right will result in a professional, long-lasting finish. After all, you don't want to be repainting every few years, do you?

Priming is the step many homeowners neglect. An underlying primer coat will cover stains and minor imperfections and enhance the final color. I know most people don't even want to think about painting a room twice, but unless your walls are white or a very light color and in very good shape, the result won't look right without a prior coat of primer. Professional painters use primer because it adheres to the wall surface better than paint. It also works as a sealer between the wall and the paint. Colors go on truer when you use primer beforehand. You'll save on paint in the long run because you'll use fewer coats, paint will go further, and the color will be closer to what you intended.

If painting a room a dark color, have your primer tinted to match the color you're painting. This will save you multiple coats of paint down the road. I can remember once trying to paint a room red: I needed four coats of paint to cover the walls. The next time I painted a room a dark color, I used a primer tinted the same color as the paint and only had to use a single covering of paint. Use primer just once and you'll be a believer.

The ceiling should be painted first. The traditional choice for ceilings has been white or off-white but more people are using a lighter shade of the wall color on the ceiling these days for a decorator touch. Flat paint is preferred since gloss can highlight cracks in the plaster, especially in older homes.

The baseboard trim and any chair railing on the walls comes next, then the doors and door trim, and finally the window trim. Done? Let the paint dry, then decide whether you need to do a second coat. That wasn't so hard, was it?

ASK YOUR GUIDE

How much paint do I need? Talking about square footage always confuses me.

▸ There's a handy paint calculator at www.bobvila.com that will make those manual calculations a thing of the past. Paint manufacturers and home improvement stores also have calculators on their Web sites. While it's a good idea to keep some leftover paint for touchups, there's no need to keep more than an extra gallon. Close paint cans tightly and store in the garage away from heat.

▶ To sponge paint, you'll need a paint tray, liner, and a paint roller, as well as a natural sea sponge, a bucket, stirring stick, and rubber gloves. Two colors of paint are needed: a base paint to cover the walls and a paint mixed with glaze. The most important thing to remember is not to compromise on the quality of the sea sponge, which is vital to the success of your job.

Now get out the roller and the paint brush. A paint brush is used to cut in near the ceiling, baseboards, and where the walls meet. A roller is used for more expansive surfaces. There are rollers available (next to traditional rollers in the paint store) that hold paint in a chamber so you don't have to return to the paint tray as much. Not only is this feature convenient, the holes in the roller make for a more even and easier paint application.

Decorative Painting Techniques

I have noticed that people are choosing to use paint in varied ways these days as an alternative to wallpaper. Paint is cheaper and easier to apply, and when you want to change the look, you don't have to go to the trouble of taking down wallpaper.

Vary finishes to create a pattern. You can achieve an interesting effect by applying both flat and satin paint in stripes or blocks on your wall. Tape off a section and use a roller to apply one type of paint, let it dry, then use the other type of paint on the next section of wall. The result is a subtle effect that can enhance a room for little effort and money.

Sponge painting is a simple and easy way to transform a room. Sponging gives the look of texture and depth to walls, which works for hiding cracks and other irregularities.

Begin by applying one color on the walls, then use another slightly lighter or darker color for the sponge-painting coat. Choose a lighter or darker color to sponge. Paint your walls the color you desire, let them dry, and then you're ready for the sponge painting. Lightly dip a damp sponge in paint. If you get too much paint on the sponge, blot off the excess. Practice dabbing the sponge on a piece of board or other material until you get the effect you want. Have fun with the process—the effect is meant to look random, not planned. Use a light touch as you work, and work in a random pattern for best effect. Re-dip the sponge and keep working on a small area at a time, keeping the edge of the painted area wet until you're finished. Stand back occasionally to check your progress and gauge the uniformity of the look.

Try doing a Venetian plaster effect. Many people who have visited Italy, especially the Tuscan countryside or Venice, come back talking about the wonderful color-washed walls. You can imitate the look of those time-worn walls with little time and effort and very little money. You'll need all-purpose joint compound (not the fast-drying kind that dries in twenty minutes). A five-gallon bucket will suffice for the average-size room. Then buy several colors of latex earth-tone paint—three are best.

▲ Venetian plaster technique

Mix together the first color with the joint compound in a good-sized bucket. Then use a large spackling or putty knife to apply the mixture in a swirling motion to the wall, trying not to spread it on too thick. Then while the first layer is still wet, do the same with the second color of paint, overlapping and swirling for the effect you want. Repeat with a third color for a truly rich effect. The top color will be the dominant one.

If you want to spend a little more money and not work with the joint compound, there are products such as Venetian Plaster made by Behr Paint. This comes in various colors ready to use. Whether you use the do-it-yourself technique with joint compound or a ready-made plaster from a paint manufacturer, the effect will be unique. Information on this and other faux painting techniques is available on my About.com site and by typing *faux painting technique* into an Internet search engine.

Paint stencils or a mural instead of using wallpaper. If you've ever had to strip off old wallpaper, especially having to remove more than one layer, you may never want to put it up again. Instead think about creating the same look by using paint. You can create stripes, squares, flowers, clouds—just about anything you can imagine. Don't like the result? Just repaint.

Paint can also be used to mimic stone, stucco, and tile. Want to brighten your kitchen with some tile but don't want the expense or hassle? Just faux paint some tiles. I once faux painted two columns in a living room to look like marble, and they were stunning.

When You Don't Want to Paint

If you've decided not to go all the way with paint (say, your landlord doesn't want color on the walls, or you prefer the white-wall look), there are other good ways to add color to a room. The use of accent walls, fabrics, and accessories are easy ways to add color without taking on a large painting project.

Try painting just one wall first. This changes the focal point of the room without turning into a major makeover. Which wall? Well, if the room has a fireplace, try painting walls adjacent to it. Because a fireplace is a natural focal point, nearby color will draw the eye to this area. If you have a display niche, that's also a perfect place for some extra color. I like to use a bold, contrasting color from a fabric in the room, or a subtle hue either a shade lighter or darker than the color of other walls in the room.

Choose colorful fabrics. Nothing adds color to a room like beautiful fabric, whether in a solid or print. I recommend choosing your fabrics first, since paint is so easy to match. Sometimes I get inspiration for a color for walls or furnishings from a fabric, and sometimes the fabric inspires the paint color. If you find a multicolored fabric that's especially pleasing, select its predominant color or one that speaks to you and match the paint to it.

Fabrics come in diverse textures as well as colors, including silk, linen, moiré, eyelet, acetate, ticking, gingham, and muslin. Some of the synthetic fabrics look like the real thing but cost less and often have a fabric finish, which means easier care and no ironing.

Use fabric to add color to upholstery, window treatments, and accessories. Photos can be placed on fabric and framed to create an unusual background. Fabric can also be used to edge simple rugs or even to make those rag rugs used in country decorating. Use fabric tassels to tie curtains back, or try the many types of fringe on the market to embellish fabrics and put your own imprint on a room.

Accessories offer a special opportunity to add color. A decorative lamp is a good place for color, such as through an artful Tiffany reproduction lamp. You can have an interesting pot or sculpture wired and turned into a lamp. A good lamp shop can do the job for a reasonable price. Add a shade in an interesting shape or color and top with fringe, beads, or ribbon. Now you have a colorful lamp that is an original.

Art is always a striking way to add color, drama, and interest to a room. Try one large painting or a collection of smaller ones in interesting shapes and frames. I like to take photos to a framing shop where I can choose mats in dozens of colors from pastel to bright and vary the types of frames. Then I group the photos on a wall or on a table for a dramatic effect.

Color stands out on a floor—and you don't have to have brand-new wall-to-wall carpet. Just use a colorful throw rug on whatever kind of floor you have. There are hundreds of types of area rugs from florals to patterns in all kinds of interesting textures and shapes. The right rug can transform the decorating style of a room. I had a client who wanted to try contemporary in her living room but didn't want to buy new furniture. We found a lively rug with contemporary blocks of color that gave the room real style for very little money.

Reflect the color in the room by hanging a large mirror, ideally one with an interesting frame. Or redo a mirror you already have with new paint or cording, braid, or silver or gold foil, available at craft stores. People are always surprised at how a mirror enhances a room with light and color.

Toss a throw on a sofa for instant color, texture, and comfort. Choose a color that's a contrast or accent for maximum effect. Just see how quickly you use a quilt to snuggle up with a book or a movie on a favorite chair.

Bring in Mother Nature with some natural color by way of plants and flowers. A glorious arrangement of blooms from a florist or grocery store adds fragrance and personality to a room. A ficus tree in front of a window or a palm in a room decorated with an island theme contributes a wonderful touch. If you don't have a green thumb, take a look at the realistic silk flowers available, needing only a dusting now and then.

Get Linked

Articles on color are especially popular on my Interior Decorating site on About.com. For people afraid to be bold or daring, the following links can help with choosing colors.

TOP ONE-COLOR DECORATING SCHEMES

If you're stuck with white walls or actually love the crisp, clean look of white or off-white, see how bringing in one other color can create a dramatic color scheme.

http://about.com/interiordec/onecolor

HOW TO CHOOSE THE RIGHT COLOR PAINT

If you have a good sense of color, you're very fortunate. It can be difficult to match shades of green or blue, for instance. If you're not sure how to select the right color for your room, you'll find some good tips in this article.

http://about.com/interiordec/choosepaint

FROM FASHION WEEK TO LIVING ROOM CHIC

Read about how fashion designers set the tone for interior decorating colors and how interior designers incorporate runway fashions and color combinations into home decorating.

http://about.com/interiordec/fashion

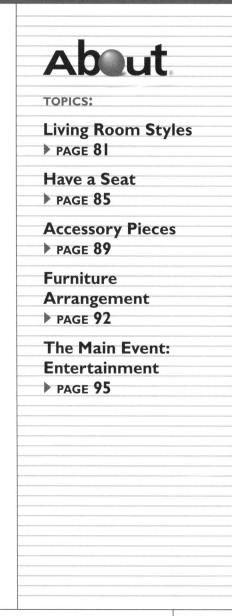

Chapter 7

Your Living Room

Living Room Styles

Perhaps you're thinking about redecorating your living room. The way you use this room may have changed. It may be that for a long time you were busy with small children, but they've gotten older or since left the nest. Now you have more time to entertain, and you want the living room to be the place for this. Maybe you have had a formal living room and currently want an informal one—or vice versa. Whatever the reason you're looking into redecorating, the living room is a central room and will probably require spending significant time and money redoing it. Planning is vital.

So this is the time to use a decorating file and work out your design plan. Think about your life and what your needs are now and for the foreseeable future. Which style will work best: formal or informal? Which aspects of each do you like? Each sets a certain mood and serves a certain need. Do you like the tradition and orderliness of a formal living room? Or do you like having an informal space where people feel free to put their feet on the coffee table?

I inherited some very good formal furniture for my living room, but I have a really informal family room. What should I do?

▶ You are fortunate to have some pieces of furniture you don't have to buy. Put a more casual cover on the sofa, either by reupholstering or through a slipcover. Add pillows in fun prints. Put a tablecloth over one of a pair of matching side tables or a new shade on one lamp. Without matching pairs, things will naturally look more informal.

A formal living room conveys that you like tradition and elegance. Décor in a formal living room is often symmetrical. You'll see a sofa with a painting above it and an end table on either side. The idea is to create an orderly, neat appearance.

Formal needn't be expensive. If you choose a few good pieces of furniture, move them into a traditional symmetrical arrangement, and use rich fabrics on upholstery and window treatments, you have the beginning of a wonderful formal room. If your home has an entry or foyer, set the mood to enter the formal living room by using a wonderful chest or table with some silver-framed photos, a vase of flowers, and perhaps a small Oriental rug. A room can be made more formal by using more luxurious fabrics on the furniture and for the window coverings. Silks, satins, tapestry fabrics—anything that is rich (and usually costs more!) makes a room more formal. Many formal living rooms (and dining rooms, even bathrooms these days) feature crystal chandeliers. A leather sofa or chair can work in a formal living room as long as it doesn't look too informal. Some furniture stores cater to furnishings for either formal or informal living rooms, if not both. Furniture stores provide valuable decorating ideas on how to feature favorite pieces in your home. Choose well-made pieces in formal styles that will last a long time, such as a Chesterfield sofa and wing chairs made of high-quality wood and covered in rich fabric. Add a Persian or Oriental carpet on a hardwood floor or choose a high-grade wall-to-wall carpet. Crown molding completes your formal living room.

Today's informal living room has softer lines, fewer rules, more color. Symmetry isn't as important here as it is in formal living rooms. Selection and placement of furniture is less structured, with one exception: Seating is commonly arranged around the television set or the fireplace. Ever-larger television sets using high-definition technology are very often the focal point of the living room, frequently housed in a big entertainment unit.

▲ Living room furniture arranged around a fireplace

A coffee table that you can put your feet upon without hurting the finish is a must in today's informal living room. There may even be a desk for the ever-present computer. An ottoman placed next to a comfortable chair also offers a place to put your feet up. Furniture should not be placed in a symmetrical, ordered arrangement like in formal rooms. The sofa is always placed so that the television is in easy-viewing range. Group a few chairs for a conversation area. Make sure the upholstery on the sofa and chairs is easy-care since you don't want to worry about stains. Although furniture doesn't have to be matched or expensive, it should be well-made since your family relaxing in that room will give it a lot of wear and

TOOLS YOU NEED

▶ It's a good idea to buy furniture that can serve several purposes. An armoire can store games, hobby supplies, books, homework, and office supplies. A long table can serve as desk, dining table, hobby headquarters, and gathering place. An ottoman is good for resting feet and using as a coffee table. A small chest houses linens, mittens and gloves, clothes, and miscellany. By buying furniture with many uses, it will always have a place in your home.

tear. Flooring can be wall-to-wall carpeting (Berber stands up well) or a big area rug over hardwood floors.

Do you have a combination living room/dining room?
This more open floor plan became popular when people began building larger homes with fewer walls between rooms. Before central heating became available, it was prudent to have smaller rooms that you could heat or not depending on whether they were used. With the advent of building technology and a more modern style of architecture after World War II, rooms expanded, walls came down, and a more open, airy space became popular. The formal decorating style didn't go away with this style of room layout, but it does seem to have become a little more casual.

If you have a living/dining combination room, take advantage of the flowing space. Don't break up the space by painting each room a different color. By using one color throughout, the space will look more open and airy. If the room is too large, painting just one wall a slightly different color will close up the space some. Living/dining rooms can be trickier to decorate than two separate rooms because you have to put some thought into how the two rooms flow together, but it's well worth the effort.

The furniture arrangement for a living/dining room depends on the size and shape of the room. If the room is exceptionally long and rectangular, you'll want to group your living room furniture to define a conversation space. Putting down an area rug—even an area rug over wall-to-wall carpeting—will center or ground the space as a living room setting. Sometimes a **chaise lounge** or two chairs can be placed to separate the two rooms. Living room and dining room furniture don't have to match but they should definitely coordinate in a pleasing manner. This isn't a setup for having rustic furniture in the living room and Oriental in the dining room.

The hottest change in home design involves a redesign of the family room. With families busier than ever, it has become more important to multitask at home, not just at the office. So the wall has come down between the kitchen and the family room in older homes. The open space enables anyone cooking in the kitchen to enjoy seeing what's going on in the family room. In newer homes, an island separates the kitchen from the living room or the family room. This feature comes in handy in the morning. Mom and Dad can get breakfast for the kids who sit at the island making plans for school. Later in the day when the family reconverges at home, kids can sit at the same island, do their homework, and have a snack while a parent cooks.

Use easy-to-clean fabrics or washable slipcovers on sofa and chairs in the family room and on barstools arranged around the island. And speaking of barstools: If you have small children, is that island going to be so high that you fear for their safety every time they clamber upon the stools? If so, consider having a lower section of island where children can be seated safely. Using washable paint makes practical sense on any painted island that kids might accidentally kick, leaving scuff marks. Most countertops these days are family-friendly, although you should ask your installer whether the granite countertop you want will work with younger children. Contrary to what some people think, granite isn't as tough as it looks and can be damaged with careless use.

Have a Seat

Let's face it: The two main positions we find ourselves assuming in the living room are sitting and reclining. Whether you're watching TV, reading a book, or taking a nap, you need a place to sit or lie down. For this purpose, most people furnish their living rooms with some combination of sofas and chairs.

There are many types of sofas available. The large selection can seem overwhelming, but this is really just a matter of figuring out what works for your space and how you'll use it. Here's an overview:

- **Tuxedo sofa:** This is an overstuffed sofa that has upholstered arms. A tuxedo sofa can have either a straight rectangular shape, or it can curve slightly at both ends.
- **Sofabed:** This sofa has a hidden bed that can be pulled out. These are convenient for overnight guests.
- **Sectional sofa:** This sofa gives the look of a big sofa but you can separate it to create different room arrangements and to make moving easier.
- **Chaise:** The chaise was once called a fainting couch in the eighteenth and nineteenth centuries because ladies would lie down on them when they were having a "spell." A chaise combines a comfortable chair with a built-in ottoman; sometimes chaises have arms though often not.
- **Loveseat:** This is a smaller sofa that can seat two people. Often a loveseat is paired with a matching sofa to take the place of several **armchairs** in a living room.

If you're in the market for a sofa, the first thing I recommend is to browse through magazines and clip out photos of the type of sofa you like. When you visit a furniture store, you'll be able to describe what you're looking for and save time in the search. Typically, people replace a sofa every seven to ten years, so it's important that you pick one that will last. Construction is crucial. Does the one you like have a good support system? What are the cushion and upholstery materials? Many people were glad to see horsehair filling go by the wayside, giving way these days to sofas constructed of nonallergenic foam and fiberfill. Sofa prices

▶ **EARTHY COLORS** in the natural wood ceiling and moss green paint combine with rush, wicker, and stone for warm comfort.

▶ THERE'S NO COLOR SCHEME that looks cleaner and fresher than blue and white. You can use almost any color for accents to break the mold.

◀ CLASSIC GEORGIAN DETAILS, a Queen Anne server, and clean white trim on all the woodwork give this entry a welcoming feeling.

▲ IT'S THE STRUCTURAL ELEMENTS
that draw the eye in this room. The brick
fireplace and log storage space give a cozy
feeling. Notice the old trunk used as a coffee
table and the iron screens on the mantle.

▶ A CUSHY OTTOMAN
set on an oriental rug serves
as a coffee table and footrest
in this small space.

▶ **A WONDERFUL FARM TABLE**, painted chairs with rush seats, a colorful oriental rug, and a wonderful old light fixture show how you can pull different looks together in one room. See how the dining space is set off by the darker paint in the adjoining foreground room.

▲ CHAIRS IN THE DINING ROOM
don't have to match the table perfectly.
Combining styles of furniture just
makes the space more interesting.
Each piece stands on its own.

▶ IS THERE
ANYTHING more
wonderful than
welcoming the day
with Danish and fruit
on an outdoor porch?

▶ NOTICE HOW THE COLORS and trim join the two very separate rooms. For privacy, the doors can be closed. Different area rugs separate the spaces.

are coming down even as quality remains about the same. I've found good sofas from $400 up. As with anything else, price does not necessarily equal quality. I've seen sofas priced at $2,000 that were no better than those marked at one quarter the price. You can save on sofas by asking about floor models or discontinued models. Sometimes a floor model just needs a little spot cleaning to look brand-new. My advice is to set your budget and don't even consider pieces that will break it.

▲ A comfortable and stylish sofa and chair set

ELSEWHERE ON THE WEB

▶ Home Depot's www.home mag.com has an article with useful information on what to look for when buying a big-ticket item like a sofa. Before you buy, do you know how long it will take to have the sofa delivered? What if you don't like it after it's delivered? Most important, is there a warranty on your sofa? For how long? For which elements of the sofa?

If there's no budget for a good-quality new sofa, think about getting the one you have reupholstered. Keep in mind that between the purchase of new fabric, repairing or replacing old cushions, and the labor involved, reupholstery can be as expensive (if not more so) than buying a sofa off the floor of a showroom.

▶ Designers have loved making unusual shapes with chairs through the years. I've seen a chair shaped like red lips, ones for children shaped like fruits and vegetables, and others sculptural marvels of plastic. Remember butterfly chairs—those metal-frame chairs across which is stretched a butterfly-shaped piece of fabric? They periodically reappear as retro furniture becomes hotter. Cushionless chairs of rattan or wicker have become popular too.

But you will get just what you want. Ask an upholsterer to come to your home for an estimate or take a photo of the piece, a swatch of the fabric you've chosen, and a cushion with you to the workroom. Look at other work the reupholsterer has done. Do prints match from cushion to foundation? Are stripes running in the right direction? Has he neatly finished the underside as well as the visible areas?

If you decide to have a sofa reupholstered, you might want to update its look, such as getting rid of a skirt or having arms made more angular. This is the time when you can change not only the style but try one of the newer fabrics like microfiber. Or you might want to try a patterned sofa if you've always had a solid one (or vice versa). Here's your opportunity to make other adjustments or add embellishments like cording or trim. Beware: Any change to the original style or shape will add big bucks to the cost of the job. You might think about investing in a set of slipcovers to change the look for the seasons or as protection. As long as the upholsterer is cutting material for the reupholstering, it's easy to cut two sets instead of one.

Mass-produced slipcovers or sofa covers are another option and relatively inexpensive. I've found them for around $100. If you have slipcovers made by an upholsterer the price will vary depending on your fabric and the labor. Fewer people are becoming upholsterers these days as furniture prices drop, so you may have trouble even finding someone. If you can afford it, it's of value to have a set of slipcovers or a sofa cover to reduce wear and tear on your sofa, especially when you have young children or houseguests. Some people I know have slipcovers they bring out in the summer for a more informal look. Remember that custom slipcovers may not fit a different sofa when you replace yours.

Armchairs are another way to add decorating style to a living room. Armchairs cost less than a sofa and can add that decorating touch you're seeking. Perhaps you want to introduce a more serene Oriental theme to your living room. Choose some chairs that echo that look in line and color and add a few accessories. You'll have your theme without spending much money.

Chairs are also a smart place to introduce color. Maybe you love red, but a red sofa isn't practical; you're afraid you'll get overwhelmed with that much color in the room or tired of it. Add a red chair and you have your pop of color. You can have an armchair reupholstered for less money than you can a sofa.

Armchairs are useful for making a conversation area in a room. Put two together and you have a place for family or friends to gather. I like to place one in a corner with a lamp for a reading nook.

Do you have a fireplace? Place chairs across from each other in front of the fireplace to create a cozy place to sit. (Furniture arrangement is discussed later in this chapter.)

You can find many different types of armchairs, named for their cushioned side arms. Wing chairs have upholstered panels that extend from the upper back of the chair like wings, enveloping your shoulders as you sit, to dramatic effect in a living room. Club chairs are upholstered chairs with rounded backs like you'd see in a men's club, while side chairs are armless chairs used as dining room chairs. Throne chairs are large high-backed chairs fit for royalty. The backs of fan chairs look like unfolded fans. Slipper chairs are small, low-seated, high-backed upholstered chairs often used in bedrooms for sitting on to slip on shoes.

Accessory Pieces

A coffee table seems standard in a living room, similar to the use of end tables. The type of coffee table, end tables, and lamps will, of course, be different for different decorating styles. Use these furnishings to bring out your decorating style, taking care to avoid a cookie-cutter living room.

Coffee tables accessorize a sofa. Some people think a sofa just looks forlorn without a coffee table in front. If the original purpose of a coffee table was to hold a coffee service, today's coffee table is just as likely to be used casually to hold the TV remote, magazines, and accessories. A big rustic coffee table fits well with a leather sofa in a Western- or cabin-themed room. A wrought iron and glass table is perfect in a more feminine room. Contemporary rooms look best with something low and sleek, perhaps made of dark and shiny wood. The decorating style will dictate the type of coffee table.

End tables round off your sofa. End tables often are placed at each end of the sofa, holding a lamp and sometimes books or magazines. Many homes have a single light fixture hanging from the center of the living room, so it's important to have tables placed around the sofa for lamps. Formal rooms should have an even number of end tables (two or four) while informal rooms can have any number needed, varying in material and shape from each other.

Lamps are like sparkling earrings for a room. There are so many wonderful lamps with which to accessorize your living room that usually it's hard to keep from buying too many. But choice is good; you can hardly have enough good lighting in a living room. If you have too little, as most people do, the room can seem gloomy. On the other hand, too many bright spots of light can seem glaring. Be sure you have task lighting, meaning lamps set so you can read or do tasks. Buy a floor lamp or two to add some height in the room; lighting should never be only at table-level or ceiling-level in a room.

▲ A floor lamp placed near seating as a reading light

And make the lighting beautiful. You'll find lamps made of varied materials like pottery, crystal, and wood as well as man-made materials. Consider varied shapes, from rounded bases to tall cylinders, to add interest to a room. Overhead lighting fixtures range from rustic iron to elaborate crystal chandeliers that add elegance and drama to a room. A charming Cinderella lamp can establish a theme for a little girl's room while enabling her to read a storybook at night.

ELSEWHERE ON THE WEB

▶ The Interior Arrangement and Design Association (IADA) Web site is www .interiorarrangement.org. Each IADA member has been trained and certified to do makeovers. Read more about this professional association, learn how they work, and find a designer in your area. As with any professional you might engage, you should ask exactly about what they'll do and what fee they'll charge. The transformation they bring to a room is likely to be far less expensive than buying new furniture you may not even need.

Area rugs are a significant accessory. I love to use area rugs to add color, texture, and personality to a room. Smaller than room-sized, these can be placed on a hardwood or tiled floor or on top of wall-to-wall carpeting to define an area of color and interest.

Whichever is the design of your room, the rug should reflect that design. An earth-toned, block-patterned area rug adds drama to a contemporary room, whereas a floral rug contributes a lovely touch to a shabby chic or country cottage decorating style. (Area rugs are discussed further in Chapter 14.)

Create storage options with your accessories. If your room is small or storage is a problem, try a grouping of four small cube storage units that can be filled with magazines or blankets. I've seen ones that can be used for seating as well. Some fit under a coffee table and can be pulled out so that the unit becomes a small dining table for impromptu meals.

One table that's become popular has a lever that allows it to be easily raised for dining and lowered to be used as a coffee table. That way you can do office work or have a meal on it in its raised position without having to bend down to a coffee table. Another clever coffee table holds wicker baskets for all the stuff we collect, though a TV remote could get lost that way!

Furniture Arrangement

Sometimes the furniture in the living room still looks good, the paint is in fine condition, too, but you just need a change to make the place feel fresh. Maybe you simply need to move the furnishings around.

Furniture rearrangement has become a specialty of some interior decorators. In fact, there's a professional association of such designers known as the Interior Arrangement and Design Association

(IADA). The designers specialize in going into a client's home for a day and rearranging one or more rooms to look quite different, all the while using only the existing furnishings.

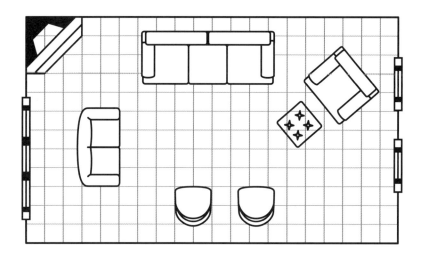

▲ A sample furniture arrangement plan

The most common decorating problem I run across is a room that has too much furniture or a mixture of styles that doesn't work. Often the designer is able to find pieces scattered throughout the house and bring them together in the room needing the makeover, which is usually the living room.

Here is a quick, easy, and inexpensive living room makeover project. First, empty the room so that you can see it anew. Then bring pieces in one at a time—slowly. Try a different arrangement from the one you've been using. I find that most people put all of their furniture against the walls. Find the focal point of the room. Is it a fireplace? The television? The view seen through a big picture window or from French doors?

Arrange the room to take advantage of the focal point. For example, place the sofa facing the fireplace so you can look out at a wonderful view.

▲ Furniture placed at an angle to add interest to the room

I find an asymmetrical arrangement to be a creative look for a living room. It will shake things up, and you might find you love the look. Instead of putting the sofa up against a wall, put it at an angle in the room and place your coffee table in front of it. Chairs can be arranged around the sofa in whichever way seems best for the type of room you have. For instance, sometimes I set the chairs in pairs to one side of the sofa or in a conversational grouping. Then situate your end tables with lamps atop them at each side of the sofa. Placing an area rug beneath the grouping of sofa and coffee table and chairs will do what decorators call anchoring—you're forming a little room within a room. Now, add pieces, but not too many. Most people have too much furniture in their rooms.

Then "shop" the other rooms in your home for accessories, putting a few of these selectively around the living room. If you're a collector, you may have parts of your collection scattered around the house. Think about bringing it together into a rearranged living room. Or if you have too much in the living room to begin with, edit the collection you're spotlighting, bringing out a few new pieces now and then and putting away objects you have previously featured. Declutter the bookcases by not filling them up entirely. Work out new arrangements of what you already have there.

Finally, bring in some plants and artwork. Try putting the art up in a different way, like at different heights, maybe even just setting it on the mantel instead of hanging it or putting it in a grouping you might not have thought of previously. There, you're finished—and you didn't spend a dime!

The Main Event: Entertainment

In the current trend of nesting at home, people are spending more time and money on home entertainment these days. With the advent of home media rooms to rival small movie theaters, more people are staying home, where you can lounge, talk as loudly as you want without being shushed, stop for a phone call, back up a scene, and make your own popcorn.

All this has created a boom for home entertainment companies that can make your living room or family room entertainment center bigger and better, complete with large-screen projection systems and movie theater-style seats, if you like.

I've seen some wonderful rooms done like a movie theater complete with curtains that open and close over the screen, comfortable chairs with drink holders, even preview movie posters on the wall. One of them had a wonderful old-fashioned popcorn popper in the corner of the room.

If you're in the market to upgrade your multimedia system or convert a room into a home entertainment center, it's important to get several estimates from highly qualified people before they come out to do the installation. It takes a professional to make all the systems compatible with each other and to do the necessary wiring. In fact, you may need to get a permit for some of the work. If the company you contact tries to downplay the need for an estimate or for a professional electrician if wiring has to be done, don't let them do the job.

Get Linked

Arranging a living room to suit the needs of your family can be a challenge. You'll find some more information about choosing furniture to suit your needs on my Interior Decorating site on About.com.

SOLVE STORAGE CHALLENGES WITH AN ARMOIRE

This versatile piece of furniture is perfect for almost any room. Read about how to use it in the living room.

http://about.com/interiordec/armoire

LOTS OF USES FOR A CHEST OF DRAWERS

Tall or short, wide or narrow, a chest of drawers is a versatile piece for a living room or family room. Read about different ways one can be used.

http://about.com/interiordec/chestdrawers

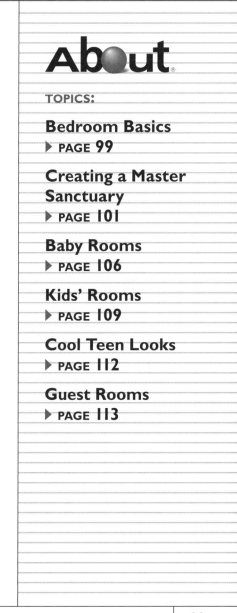

Chapter 8

Bedrooms: Not Just for Sleeping

Bedroom Basics

You've heard it so many times: We spend a third of our lives in bed. So don't you think we should have wonderful bedrooms? I do, and that's why I enjoy helping people create the kind of bedroom that leads to sweet dreams. Who are you? Are you newlyweds decorating your first bedroom together? Are you a career woman who is single? A mature married couple? A hip bachelor? A child? Who you are dictates your decorating style and needs in your bedroom.

Every bedroom needs a bed, of course, a dresser or armoire to store clothes, and one or more bedside tables and lamps. Those are the basics, like the main ingredients for a recipe. The creativity is in what you do with these. How many people will be sleeping in the bedroom? For a child's bedroom parents usually buy a twin bed, although there's no reason why you can't put in a double bed if there's room. That will give your child room to grow. If a couple

ELSEWHERE ON THE WEB

▶ It's an exercise in imagination to look at decorating books and magazines for pictures of designer bedrooms. And having a collection of beautiful books on decorating on a bookshelf or coffee table means you'll always have inspiration for your home. For the most up-to-date information about decorating, you'll find lively pictures and design ideas for bedrooms at http://bhg.com/bedrooms. Writers update the site regularly with trends and the latest fashions in decorating.

will be sleeping in the bed, buy a double, queen-, or king-sized bed, mattress, and headboard. Though some couples prefer a double bed, most people these days like the roominess of a queen or king—king-sized especially for tall people. Do you need a bedside table on each side of the bed because there are two of you? Do you want one that has drawers to store things or just a table with legs? Or maybe a round table covered with a tablecloth?

▲ An armoire used to house a TV

Televisions in the bedroom have suddenly become controversial. Some people love to watch television in bed, snuggling in to watch their favorite sitcom or maybe one of the late-night comedies. Other people can't stand to have a television in the bedroom.

They want the bedroom to be a sleeping room, not a television viewing room. You'll have to decide what's right for you.

If you do choose to have one in the bedroom, then you'll need a platform for it. Armoires have become increasingly popular in all rooms of the house, but particularly in the bedroom. They seem familiar in the bedroom, probably because they were used for storage before closets were built into homes. Now people use them for everything from storage to entertainment centers.

Creating a Master Sanctuary

With the busy lives all of us lead, it's a relief to step into our master bedroom and experience it as a sanctuary, a place of calm. If that's not the way you feel about your master bedroom, consider the following tips for transforming it into a serene setting. No matter how much money you spend, you'll cherish having a more pleasant space.

Project One: The Luxury Hotel Theme One enjoyable theme for a master suite is that of a luxury hotel. Since it's so hard to get away to a hotel for even a weekend these days, why not re-create a getaway in your own master suite?

Maybe your favorite luxury hotel has sleek, modern lines, with silver or black accents and interesting art on the walls. When you climb into bed, the sheets feel like silk, and the mattress and pillows are soft as a dream. Step into the adjoining bath and find piles of fluffy towels and a tub filled with scented bath salts. A robe of the softest terry cloth hangs on the back of the bathroom door for wrapping yourself in after your bath.

For a retreat bedroom, paint the walls a soothing pale gray. This will give the room a wonderful calm atmosphere. Then look at your headboard. You might keep your old one if it's a nice wood one that's still the look you want. If not, choose something sleek

▶ To create a hotel-style bedroom at home, think about what makes that room appealing. It starts by containing just the fundamentals. No clutter. No excess stuff. Total tranquility and order. Add a really comfortable bed, convenient bedside tables with good lighting, a bolster pillow for reading, a clock radio with CD, and an armoire with a television.

▶ Want to duplicate the look of that romantic headboard? Put a floating shelf on the wall above the bed, the kind that doesn't look like it has any support. Find one reasonably priced at hardware or home improvement stores; you can install it with little effort. Then line up some votive candles or set little crystal vases that each hold a single red rose. You've invited a romantic atmosphere into the bedroom for very little time and money.

in a dark wood or try an upholstered headboard. A silky **duvet** in gray and maroon stripes, matching fluffy towels in the master bath, a couple of hotel-plush terry robes waiting on the door, and you have that hotel luxuriousness. Hang thick draperies of matching material on the windows.

The bed is the focal point of the room and the means for feeling like you've walked into a retreat. When you visit a hotel you get away from everyday stress, especially by relaxing in a dreamy bed. Mimic that mood by dressing the bed in the most luxurious bedding you can afford. If you have a great view, situate the bed to take advantage of it when you awake. Add a comfortable loveseat to the room to feel like you have a suite, not just a single room.

▲ A luxurious bedroom

Project Two: The Romantic Bedroom Theme One of the most romantic bedrooms I've seen lately had deep, passionate red walls—the color of the roses beloved by the woman of the house. Instead of being overpowering or making the room seem smaller, this had the opposite effect. Red is a color that may require several coats of paint, even using a tinted primer, but the rich effect is well worth it. On the bed lay a cushy comforter of white eyelet and lots of accent pillows. And the centerpiece of the room was a dark mahogany headboard holding a shelf on which sat a dozen votive candles, creating a soft, romantic glow. No children allowed!

WHAT'S HOT

▶ What island bedroom would be complete without shells? If you're an island lover, maybe you have ones you've picked up on a vacation. If not, you can buy some. Place starfish on a shelf and pile shells in a bowl or basket. I like to fill a clear glass lamp with some sand and a few special shells, like a chambered nautilus. Put some pleasing prints of palm trees, flamingos, or tropical art on the walls.

▲ A romantic touch

ASK YOUR GUIDE

How can I create a canopy for my bed?

▶ Create your own canopy bed with a simple swag of fabric. Just drape a piece of fabric over the frame of a structured canopy bed or install curtain rods on the ceiling, placing one above each end of the bed. Tab-top or pinch-pleated panels can be attached to the curtain rod and fall softly to the floor. For further instructions or for more elaborate canopy treatments that are really simple to do, go to http://about.com/interiordec/canopybed.

Privacy is vitally important for invoking a romantic mood in your master suite. You don't want the outside world to mar the mood. It's hard to feel romantic if you hear traffic or your teenager's music, so think about choosing a different bedroom if the master suite isn't private enough. And for ultra privacy, hang some lined drapes the same color as the walls to keep sunshine from waking you when you sleep in.

Project Three: Getaway to the Islands An island theme is a popular one for the master suite. I like to put grass cloth wallpaper on the walls. Such natural wall coverings are applied with adhesives just like wallpaper. If you don't want to use wallpaper, paint the walls a pale yellow or aqua and put beadboard or plain paneling on the lower half of the walls. Beadboard and paneling come in sheets at home improvement stores. You can have it cut to fit, or if you're handy you can cut the proper length yourself at home. Measure your wall from the floor to the ceiling and plan for the beadboard or paneling to run about halfway up the wall from the floor. Depending on the thickness of the material and how long-lasting you want the effect, adhere it with nails and glue recommended by the manufacturer. Using the same width measurements, cut the trim and adhere the same way as the beadboard or paneling. Install bamboo blinds on the windows or try some shutters painted white. Sheers that billow in the breeze when the windows are open and an overhead paddle fan are pleasing touches. Rattan or wicker furniture fosters a light, carefree mood.

A canopy of netting is a resourceful idea for an island-themed bedroom and is inexpensive. You can usually buy a ready-made one for less than $100 in a home or import store or make a simple one yourself for even less.

An inviting look for an island-themed master bedroom is to place the bed asymmetrically in a corner beside a real or silk palm tree, giving you the feel of an island right next to the bed. If there's room, make a quiet nook to catch up on reading with a chair, ottoman, and reading lamp.

A few simple accessories can make your bathroom a part of the island-themed master suite. Continue the color of the bedroom walls into the bathroom, pile some colorful towels in a beach tote, and fill a bowl with shell-shaped soaps. I found some darling framed photographs of bright colored surfboards and used them in an island-themed bathroom for teens. Whimsical mermaids or pen and ink sketches of island cottages work too. Can you hear the sound of the surf already?

Project Four: That Country Feeling Have you visited the French countryside or always wanted to? Love a big, soft canopy bed piled with a down comforter and pillows? Do you favor colors like rose or wine? Maybe a master bedroom suite decorated in a French country style would provide a perfect sanctuary for you.

Furniture can be dark wood or painted in your color of choice. Go for lots of texture on the bed with fabrics like silk and velvet or think about using toile. Nothing conveys the mood of French country like toile. Use the print along with fabrics in contrasting plaids and stripes on the bed or just try several pillows if you don't want that much print in the room. Photos or prints of France are a must to carry out the theme. I once used a wonderful lamp shaped like the Eiffel Tower on a bedroom dresser.

This bedroom should be filled with lots of collectibles that remind you of France, rather than taking on a minimalist look. Find some attractive objects (they don't have to be antiques or even valuable) and group them on a **vanity** table or atop a dresser. A few books on France are a nice touch on a bedside table. Use lacy curtains at the windows or continue the toile pattern from the bed

ASK YOUR GUIDE

My husband and I have decided not to learn the sex of our baby before it's born, but we want the nursery ready for the big day. What colors should we use?

▶ Happily, baby rooms don't have to be pink or blue anymore. I love a nursery with soft taupe or sand-colored walls because it emphasizes delicate baby colors. Add blankets, toys, and accessories in the colors of your choice when the baby arrives. Or choose a soft butter yellow and make additions later.

on curtains or a **valance** at the windows. If you have French doors, even better. Remember to introduce French scents too. Bring in lots of flowers, which the French love for color and fragrance. Pot-pourri, especially lavender, will enhance the mood.

Add a French touch to a bathroom with a charming rug, plush terry towels, an iron towel rack, and a stool with rush seat, coordi-nating the color scheme around a toile fabric.

And don't forget to include a tray beside the bed serving crois-sants and hot chocolate for breakfast in bed. Or set a tray with a carafe of wine and wine glasses for a nightcap. C'est magnifique!

Baby Rooms

I love working on a baby's room. Here dreams really do come true. If you have a baby on the way, one of the things on your mind is sure to be where the baby will sleep and how you'll decorate that space. Each baby is special, so you want to have a nursery that reflects that. It's time to get out your decorating file and work on your design plan.

It's easier to decorate a baby's room if you have a theme or color palette in mind. You probably chose one not long after you found out you were pregnant and tucked ideas away in your decorating file. If you don't want to have to change the room just a few years after you decorate, think about a theme that will grow with the baby. For instance, a sports theme for a boy's room could last through the teenage years whereas a teddy bear theme wouldn't.

Some parents like to decorate according to gender. Popular themes for a boy's room are early versions of those for older chil-dren, such as sports themes like baseball or football. Themes for a girl's room include flowers, dolls like Raggedy Ann and Andy, and fairies. Some popular themes for baby's rooms are animal themes such as Noah's Ark or zoo animals; storybook characters such as Winnie the Pooh; baby animals such as bunnies, ducklings, and baby penguins; and Disney characters. These themes are unisex but can be made more gender-specific depending on the wall colors you use. Crib bedding, wall decorations such as stencils and murals, even paint in Disney-approved colors are available in children's stores.

Speaking of colors, even though red is the first color that babies see, you probably don't want to paint the nursery in such an eye-opening shade. Babies love primary colors rather than pastels, but bright blue, red, or yellow might not be to your taste. Don't worry. Your baby is going to love his room however you decorate it.

The most important piece of furniture in the room is, of course, the baby's crib. There are so many different styles of cribs: canopies, wood-carved, wrought iron, and rainbow-colored. There are cribs that have Plexiglas windows so a baby can see out and cribs with animals painted on them. You can even choose a crib that converts to a **daybed**, then a youth bed, and finally to a bed that can last through the teenage years (if you have the budget for this expensive piece of furniture). Add an armoire and you won't have to buy furniture for the child again. In fact, when your child moves out of the family home, she'll have a bed and armoire to take with her to her first apartment.

In selecting a crib, start with safety, of course. Is the finish on the wood smooth? Is the railing easy for you to move down, though not for the baby? Is the crib of good quality? How about assembly? Will you want to do that yourself or pay for it to be done? (This is just the start of facing the "some assembly required" aspect of a child's pieces in the coming years.) Do you want the crib to be part of a set or to buy furniture pieces individually?

While your child is little you'll probably want to place the crib where you can see the baby without entering the room. That way

With all these toys everywhere, I feel like the room décor gets lost. What can I do?

▶ When my girls were young, they loved dolls and stuffed animals. (Surprise!) But I liked to have these off the floor when they weren't being used. I found a wonderful antique infant crib without rockers that worked perfectly. My dad refinished the spindles, the toys were lined up beautifully, and the clutter was off the floor. It looked much nicer than a toy box.

you can check on him without letting him think it's time to get up. (You might have just put him down.) Of course, you should check for any drafts from air conditioning vents or windows. It's best not to place a crib near a window, not just because of drafts but also because of safety issues: There have been babies who have climbed out of their cribs and fallen out a nearby window.

Associated with the crib is the matter of mattress and bedding. Your baby spends a lot of time sleeping in her crib, so a nice firm mattress is important. A new baby can't raise her head, so a soft mattress could pose a suffocation hazard. As for bedding, you can choose whatever you think goes best with the theme you've picked. And don't think you can get away with having just a few sets as you do for your own bed—have at least half a dozen for the inevitable accidents. Bumper pads should have tabs or securely fastened ties to hold them against the crib so that baby doesn't hurt her head when she moves around.

There are a few other items you might want in your baby's room. For one thing, a changing table is a must. Some baby furniture sets come with a changing table that matches the crib, dresser, and armoire. Dressers intended for infant rooms often have convertible tops so that a baby can be changed safely on top of a pad. Later the top can be removed and the piece used as a child's dresser.

And don't forget the accessories. A lamp can do a lot to give a nursery some character, such as using a giraffe lamp to complement a Noah's Ark theme. If you install some shelves high on the wall, they'll provide a place for putting photos and objects out of the child's reach. A toy chest is essential for a child's room. So, too, is a rocking chair for those precious times when you rock the baby to sleep or have a late-night feeding. Don't forget that all-important nightlight so you can check on baby without waking him.

Babies have a lot of stuff. Where are you going to store it all? Use pretty baskets and covered boxes to hide all those things on shelves, in armoires, bookcases, and closets. These are inexpensive and help to neaten a room. While the baby is still in a crib, you can even put some wicker baskets under the crib for storage. As the baby grows, you can use decorative boxes to store keepsakes.

Kids' Rooms

Once upon a time, kids' bedrooms held a little of this, a little of that. The kids got hand-me-downs from the parents' bedroom, even castoffs of extended family. The walls would be pink for girls (maybe lavender) and blue for boys. Frilly curtains hung at the windows for girls, plain panels for boys. There was the mandatory picture of a ballerina for the girls and sports memorabilia for the boys.

Times have changed. Families are smaller these days and more of them consist of two working parents. In many homes there's more income and more interest in decorating. Is it any wonder that kids, like adults, want comfort and style in their rooms? Remember, it's the one place in the home that is wholly their own.

Children love imagination and fantasy. That is why themes are so fitting for kids' rooms. Whether your daughter wants a bedroom like Cinderella or your son wants a pirate's lair, let them help plan and do as much of the work as possible on their rooms to make them truly theirs.

Remember the fun you've had keeping a decorating file? Let your child create one, too. If your kids don't know right away what they want for a theme, help them look in their favorite books and magazines or go online to do some research. Fabric, wallpaper, or border paper can reinforce a theme you both choose. Choosing a themed wallpaper border can cut down the work of wallpapering a whole room. This is also easily changed as your child gets older

TOOLS YOU NEED

▶ Have some fun and create a special headboard for your child's bed. With just a few simple tools and materials, you can do the job yourself. Just assemble a piece of wood (your lumber store can cut it to order), foam and batting, fun decorative fabric, a staple gun, and a simple pattern you can make or buy. There are directions, even videos to show you how on www.hgtv.com.

▶ Try out the new paint that can turn a portion of wall into a chalkboard. It's excellent for scribbling on. Just follow the directions on the can and after it dries, your child (or you) can draw pictures or write reminders on it. There's even a magnetic paint for putting up artwork and notes. Bulletin boards and cork boards have taken on new shapes and colors as well.

and wants to redecorate, as are stencils that can be painted over. Gather paint chips as well to help decide on colors.

Kids need basic furniture. First and foremost is the bed. There's no end to the varied styles for beds these days. Once bunk beds looked like military- or dormitory-issued structures. Today they're built as castles and playhouses. A smart way to conserve space is to install a **loft bed**, which leaves a space underneath the raised bunk to accommodate a desk or big comfy chair—or if left bare can leave room to play. Try a **trundle bed** to allow a second bed for sleepovers without taking up extra space.

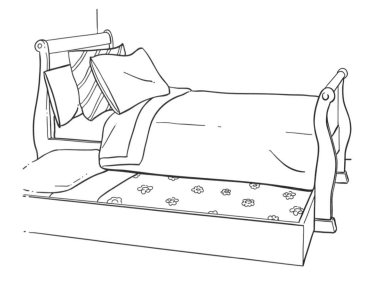

▲ A trundle bed is great for sleepovers

Kids' beds come in all shapes and sizes. Some come with ready-made themes. Here are just a few of the playful beds for children you can buy today:

- Race-car bed
- Sports-themed bed
- Castle loft bed
- Cartoon-themed bed
- Sailboat bed
- Covered-wagon bed

You get the idea. Many of these styles can be duplicated if you're handy.

There are a few other pieces of furniture your child needs. Your child requires some sort of dresser to keep her clothes in. Make sure she also has a desk so there's a designated place for homework. You can buy a desk that matches your theme or color scheme, or you can paint one yourself. Add a lamp to the desk and one to a bedside table for reading. A bookcase is essential, as is some type of storage for toys and all the gear kids accumulate.

What about linens? For starters, bedding for kids should be easy to care for, durable, and above all fun. If painting the walls is not an option, you can add a theme, color, and texture with a vivid bedspread or comforter. Try one of the bed-in-a-bag sets for a coordinated look at a good price. I tell parents that it's a good idea not to spend too much on the bedspread or comforter, both because accidents happen and kids' tastes change. If you haven't spent too much on bedding, you'll be able to give it away without feeling too extravagant.

Keep the window treatments simple: blinds, panel curtains, or café curtains. Some bedspread and comforter sets come with curtains. Think about doing a valance atop the blinds. It doesn't take

TOOLS YOU NEED

▶ The teen years are a delicate balance between childhood and adulthood. This is the time to get rid of childish things and add more adult themes. You can sometimes use the same paint color for the walls you've used for years, but change from cartoon-themed bedding to solids or sophisticated patterns. Pack up the toys, but keep the storage container for sports equipment, hobbies, and school supplies. I have a whole list of things to do to make a child's room more sophisticated at http://about.com/interiordec/teenrooms.

much time and effort to make a simple one. A feminine girl's room looks adorable with frilly Priscilla or lace curtains.

Finally, add some finishing touches to your child's room. If you have wooden floors, think about using an area rug for color and texture. There are so many ones made especially for a child's room, it will make you dizzy. I like those marked with a game for kids to play or a track for toy cars to follow.

Top it off with some art to match the theme. You can either buy this ready-made or else frame some art your child has done. Cut out pictures and photos from books and frame them yourself inexpensively.

Cool Teen Looks

If you've discovered that your child enjoys a place of his own, wait until you have a teenager! I've found that teenagers really need a place where they can get away from their world's hustle and bustle. Teens love a big room just like everyone, but if you can give them only a small space to make their own, do it. Very few teens enjoy sharing a room with a sibling. Everyone will be happier if you can work out a solution for individual privacy, even if you just put up a partition of fabric or plywood to make separate areas.

That color your child loved when younger is now, of course, so uncool. So it's time to redo the room. What with all those expenses for clothes and extracurricular activities, you're probably wondering how on earth you can afford to redecorate your teenager's room.

I've found teens like more dramatic colors than younger kids. You might even have a teen who wants to paint the walls black, though that is where I'd draw the line! If black seems too much to you as well, you can compromise by painting just one wall as an accent. If your teen likes to put up posters, as many do, a neutral wall color might be best. You can either continue that neutral color on bedding or else decide to emphasize color there. It's up to your teen. He definitely should have the room look the way he wants. (Maybe then he'll actually keep it clean.)

Teens can learn valuable life skills by helping to design their bedrooms. Here they get to express their individuality, have their needs respected, and learn to work on a project with parents. Introducing the reality of a budget is a very valuable concept. As elsewhere in life, we can't have everything we want in a bedroom. Knowing that there is a set sum allotted for the project teaches a child to make choices. Does your daughter want that expensive bed? Then there won't be as much money for bedding or for other pieces of furniture. Maybe the lesson of not getting everything at once is a good one. If hand-me-down furniture is used, paint it all one color to give a coordinated look and make the prospect of new furniture something to look forward to later. An individual piece or an entire set can be given as a gift for a birthday or holiday. Recruit your teen to also do some of the physical work to decorate the room. Even a young child can wield a paint brush, help in preparing the work space, or cleanup afterward.

Guest Rooms

If you love to have houseguests, as I do, you'll want to make your guest room as inviting as possible. Remember that guests need a place to set their suitcase down, a space cleared in the closet, and hangers to hang their clothes on. A drawer or two is appreciated as well. And, above all, guests need privacy. Make sure you have an arrangement that can give it to them.

A standard option is a basic adult guest room. Think about the way you've decorated the rest of your house. Do you want to continue the design you've got in the rest of the house (like traditional, contemporary, country) in the guest room? Or do you want it to look totally different, like a hotel or a room in a bed and breakfast? Decide on your design plan before you do anything else.

▲ A warm, inviting guest room with adjoining bathroom

Then as a first step in redecorating, give the walls a fresh coat of paint. Choose a color that is soft and soothing (like a pastel or neutral tone rather than a bright one) so your guests will be able to relax in the room. Then buy a new comforter and new bed linens to match. Be sure to have a table with a lamp on each side of the bed so your guests can read before going to sleep. Since your guests will be unfamiliar with the room and you don't want any accidents, make sure you don't have any area rugs they could trip on at night. This is especially important if you have elderly guests coming. Artwork can be any photo or painting that coordinates with the room. Or this could be the place to showcase photos of your family celebrating holidays and traveling. After all, if these are guests you invite into your home, they'll want to see these photos. They might even be in them.

You don't have to buy all new things. Just remember to make the guest room as fresh and inviting as you can, maybe with a beautiful color on the walls or a floral comforter on the bed. Your guests will feel welcome when they stay in the room.

Matters are a little different when you have little guests in your home. A perfect room for grandchildren would include a crib or a child-size bed, depending on the age and size of the child. When children are little, folding portable cribs work well. You can set them up easily and keep them stored in the bedroom closet when not in use. Later you can add a bigger bed as the children grow. It's best not to place a child's bed near a window lest children pull down curtains or fall out the window. Child-proof the room and be sure to provide a toybox filled with age-appropriate toys.

Do you have a guest room that doubles as a workout room? While it makes decorating a bit of a challenge, this is actually a good way to get maximum use out of a room. The key here is to make the workout portion feel as separated as possible from the guest room portion. Try using a screen to hide exercise equipment and to ensure safety. You don't want someone tripping over a machine in the middle of the night.

A combination guest room/home office is another common arrangement. Place the bed on the opposite side of the room from the office—the size and shape of the room will dictate the best room arrangement. If the room is small, consider putting a smaller-sized bed in the room so you won't feel overwhelmed by furniture. Try to situate your desk on one wall near a window so you can get good natural light and occasionally look out at a view.

Another worthwhile idea for an office/guest room is to place an armoire along the longest wall in the room. Open the doors of the armoire and create bulletin boards on the inside of the doors by measuring, cutting, and gluing cork bulletin board or fabric-covered board. Place your laptop computer on the shelf where a television would normally go and the printer on the shelf below. On the shelf above, place wicker baskets for paperwork. There! You have an office in your guest bedroom, one you can shut away inside the armoire by closing the doors.

You might also want to try a combined hobby/guest room. If you love to sew, let this hobby create the theme for the room. Set up a corner with your sewing machine on a table, make colorful displays with baskets of spools of thread and trims, and use quilts—homemade or purchased—on the bed and on the wall above the bed as beautiful wall hangings. If your hobby is collecting, display those collections of china figurines or teapots on shelves around the room and coordinate the bed covering to match. Maybe your hobby is playing video games. A design plan of gray walls, a sleek black metal bed and side tables, and a red bedspread will set a modern tone.

Get Linked

On my Interior Decorating site, I have pictures of beautiful bedrooms for all ages and handy ideas for creating personal spaces. The links here will give you inspiration.

DECORATING IDEAS FOR BOYS' ROOMS

I've listed some of the most popular themes for boys' rooms and given you ideas on how to use toys, colors, and accessories to enhance the look.

http://about.com/interiordec/boythemes

DECORATING IDEAS FOR GIRLS' ROOMS

Don't forget the girls! Check out this link for some popular themes for girls' rooms.

http://about.com/interiordec/girlthemes

PUT TOGETHER THE PERFECT GUEST ROOM

If you're like me, you want your houseguests to be really comfortable. My article offers ideas on things to do to create a comfortable home-away-from-home for your visitors.

http://about.com/interiordec/guestroom

Chapter 9

Beautiful Bathrooms

Decorating Styles

Whether large or small, bathrooms are a lot of fun to decorate. Even if your bathroom is large, decorating it doesn't usually take as much time or money as it does for other rooms. And unless you're planning a major remodel that includes ripping out fixtures, it probably won't be as expensive as that of a kitchen.

Have you recently redecorated or remodeled your master bedroom? Then continue its color, style, and fabric in the master bath. Get out your decorating file and envision how the paint color will look on the bathroom walls. Is the light different in that room? Chances are it is. You may have to go lighter or darker or use a different type of paint altogether. It might be that you want to use an oil-based paint instead of latex or a satin finish instead of flat. If you've used wallpaper in your master bedroom, you might be thinking of using it in the bathroom. But what about moisture? If the room is small and you love to take long, hot showers, wallpaper might start peeling from the walls.

About.

Traditional is a very popular style for bathrooms. There's something reassuring about a style we're familiar with, after all. Traditional has an orderliness that's attractive in bathrooms, often a small space. White is an obvious choice, but almond or beige are favored as well. Open the door to a traditional bathroom and you won't find a color such as dark aqua used in a tub. To create a traditional room, paint one wall as an accent with aqua or hang an aqua and cream striped wallpaper; set out towels of the same colors, and hang cream curtains at the window. Then set out aqua accessories on the vanity. Line up quality towels—perhaps monogrammed—on a towel bar. Install a new faucet in a sophisticated nickel or pewter finish or use an old-fashioned white porcelain.

WHAT'S HOT

▶ To coordinate your master bath with the master bedroom, you'll need to find colors, textures, and patterns that carry the look from one room to the next. Get out your decorating file with cuttings of fabrics and paint. Once you've decided on a color for the bathroom walls, buy a quart in the finish you want and try it on one wall. If it's too dull, move up to semigloss or gloss. The colors of the two rooms should flow but not match.

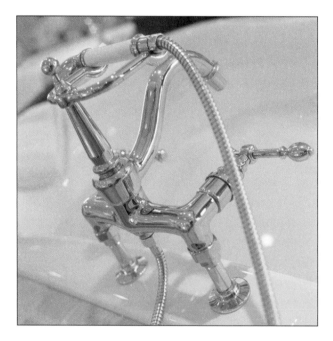

▲ New faucet for a bathtub

Here are ten easy ways to give your bathroom a traditional touch for under $100:

- Paint a classy, elegant color on the walls.
- Use a technique of painted stripes or hang subdued striped wallpaper.
- If your cabinets are light wood, stain them dark for a more traditional look.
- Frame some botanical prints and hang a grouping.
- Find a gorgeous set of silver candlesticks and fill with candles to match the room.
- Accessorize with a glass jar or dish of hand soaps and small topiaries.
- Hang a square or oval mirror with a beautiful frame with a sconce on each side.
- Replace the knobs on your vanity with new crystal knobs.
- Lay a beautiful rug in soft, tasteful colors.
- Hang a formal, traditional shower curtain in a classic stripe or subtle floral fabric.

Contemporary style is sleek, modernistic, and a little bit cool. In the bathroom this means mixing textures and materials, such as combining a vanity cabinet in a light wood with a marble or granite countertop and slate tile on the floor. Colors are earth-toned and neutral. The tub and toilet have clean, sculptural lines and faucets take on angular lines rather than a more traditional curved style. Stainless steel is used effectively in a contemporary bathroom. Lighting is subdued and unfussy, usually sculptural with clear or translucent glass. A contemporary style in bathrooms has become more familiar as many hotels and spas have adopted this look.

ASK YOUR GUIDE

My bathroom is all white and feels antiseptic. What can I do to warm it up and make it more elegant?

▶ The first thing I'd recommend is to change the lighting with a dimmer switch to change the mood from functional to relaxing. Install simple but soft window coverings and add a delicate chandelier or wall sconces. Get some thick lush towels, a candle or two, and some fragrant potpourri to transform the atmosphere of the room.

ELSEWHERE ON THE WEB

▶ Before you shop for bath fixtures, spend some time on the Internet. Major bath fixture companies like Kohler and Moen offer color and style information on their Web sites as well as give suggestions for bath design, floor layout, lighting, and flooring options. Kohler offers an online tour of its factory and has showrooms with the latest products. Visit www.kohler.com and www.moen.com for product images and decorating ideas.

Art should be modern with clean lines. Bold colors can be used in art and accessories. I used a striking triangular-shaped dresser to hold bath towels and necessities in a contemporary bathroom. The homeowner declared it her favorite piece of furniture in the whole house.

Contemporary is a good decorating style to use if you think you might be selling your home in a few years since it is popular with potential buyers. Those who don't find it to their taste can always warm up the room through the addition of color and texture.

▲ A contemporary bathroom

A romantic bathroom is another possibility. Several decorating styles fall under a romantic rubric: vintage, Victorian, country, and shabby chic. Since women spend more time in the bathroom than men, I think it's only natural that we like to decorate it in a feminine style, often in flower-toned colors like pink, blue, and green. Wallpaper is floral, curtains are usually delicate or simple, and fixtures might include an old fashioned claw-foot tub. Sometimes there's a pedestal sink or a feminine vanity with Victorian faucets.

In recent years homeowners, eager to do something different for a romantic bathroom, have cut holes in the top of old cabinets and dressers and dropped in a sink. A trend was created. Furniture and bathroom fixture manufacturers caught on quickly and now make the furniture-like cabinets with a sink installed. Some master baths feature two sinks, for him and her. Expect to pay the same as you would for a good piece of furniture.

An Easy Makeover

If you're simply looking to give your bathroom a lift without spending too much time or money, a quick, easy makeover is the route for you. Once you've decided on the wall color, take your paint chip with you to look for a new shower curtain (if you have a shower). With this relatively inexpensive item you can effect a big change in your bathroom. I remember once designing a French country master bedroom suite. After my client had spent so much money on the bedroom, she balked at the rather expensive designer toile shower curtain I showed her. It wasn't the black-and-white provincial print—she in fact loved it. After all, we'd used a similar fabric in the bedroom. But she'd always used a simple plastic shower curtain and wondered why she couldn't just do the same. I urged her to try the new curtain, and if she didn't find it perfect, I'd take it back. The minute she did, the whole room took on a different look. Some

ELSEWHERE ON THE WEB

▶ Take a look at some of the new trends in bathrooms by visiting some of the big bath showrooms online. What you'll see is color galore. Not since the 1980s have we seen such an explosion of color. But this time the colors are clearer, more vital, and vivid. I saw a red sink used in an Asian-style bathroom on one Web site. Visit www.expo.com and www.homedepot.com for product images and decorating ideas.

Can I make my own shower curtain?

▶ Yes. Next to a square tablecloth, it's one of the easiest things to make yourself, even if you are not a sewer. All you need is a flat piece of decorator fabric, lining fabric, a shower curtain liner, and some hooks. Finish the seams of the flat panel, add buttonholes for the hooks, and put it up. Even easier, find a flat sheet you like, hem it to the right length, and clip it up.

simple white curtains, a few prints on the wall, and a few accessories, and she had a French country bathroom for very little money.

Check out your tub and toilet. Even if you're not quite ready to replace them, there are things you can do to perk them up. Maybe all you need to do is put a new seat on the toilet. The obvious choice is one of the same color, but there are designer choices, too. I've seen seats decorated with everything from painted shells to flowers. I would definitely not recommend the styles in clear resin, even ones bonded with pretty motifs. (It really isn't a pleasant sight to look into a toilet bowl, even if it's clean.)

If the tub is chipped and you have been despairing, thinking you have to replace it, look into the new touchup and resurfacing products. The touchup product comes in a little jar like the white-out fluid we've all used on paper. You can find it at the hardware store. Buy the same color as the tub or mix two colors to get just the right shade for your tub.

Think about resurfacing the tub if the chipping damage is more severe. Look in the yellow pages of your phone book to find professionals who can do the work or contact a bath contractor. Apartment complex owners know all about tub resurfacing—that's how they make a bathroom (and kitchen appliances) look new for very little money. Expect to pay several hundred dollars, still a considerable savings over the cost of a new tub and labor, not to mention the demolition of having a tub pulled out of the bathroom.

If your vanity and sink are looking shabby, give them a face-lift. To brighten up a worn vanity, try a coat of paint either in a neutral or in an eye-catching color. If you're a little handy, you can cut some molding and add it to the front of the cabinet doors before you paint. Stencils are also an inexpensive, fun way to add interest to those vanity drawers. Then look at the sink. Is it an outdated color or too chipped to refinish? Maybe you're just tired of it. A new sink bowl is a quick fix that often costs less than $100. New faucets on a sink or tub are like adding a new pair of earrings or a new sparkly necklace to that little black dress you've been wearing for years.

Want to introduce more light and drama to your bathroom? Another fix that doesn't cost much but produces a lot of effect is the right mirror. You can get one in such varied shapes and sizes—round, rectangular, or square. Determine the frame around the mirror by the type of bathroom you have. Choose a beautiful carved wooden frame for a traditional bathroom or a sleek silver frame for a contemporary bathroom. Go whimsical with a frame decorated with shells for your romantic bathroom.

What is wonderful about a mirror is the way it opens up a room, making it feel bigger. Whatever the amount of light in your bathroom, the mirror will catch it and reflect it back. If you can position a mirror near a window overlooking a garden or water, you'll gain an even more dramatic look for your bath.

A Medium-Sized Remodel

Perhaps you're ready for a bigger project. You've tried all the cosmetic touches and something bigger is needed this time. You're fed up with a toilet that doesn't always want to work or a bathtub with a finish that's worn off through the years and never looks clean no matter how much you scrub it. The floor tiles are outdated and the bathroom window leaks every time it rains.

Start by replacing an outdated vanity that has an old faucet and countertop. Nothing jazzes up a bathroom like a beautiful new vanity, faucet, and countertop, especially one made of granite, marble, or a good knockoff.

▶ Why not try something new to add a dramatic flair to your bathroom? The new vessel sinks sit on the vanity countertop. They can be simple stainless steel for a contemporary bathroom, a lovely pottery bowl for a romantic bathroom, or a traditional porcelain. You can spend a little or a lot. Ty Pennington of TV's *Extreme Makeover: Home Edition* drilled a drain hole in the bottom of a stainless steel bowl and used it in his own bathroom.

New flooring can make even old bathtubs and toilets look better. Flooring can be tile, wood, or man-made materials like vinyl. Carpeting isn't recommended for the bathroom because of moisture concerns. Tiling isn't for amateurs. It's best to have this done by professionals because it's not an easy job, especially when tile has to be cut to fit.

Lighting, too, is something that has to be done by a professional electrician. Choose new fixtures at a lighting or home improvement store, letting it do the installation. Make sure the lighting fixture for the tub or shower can withstand moisture. The style of the fixture should be appropriate to the bathroom design. A chandelier is perfect to complete a traditional or romantic bathroom, while you'd choose something much less formal for a contemporary bathroom.

ELSEWHERE ON THE WEB

▶ If you love the look of patterned walls but are afraid to install wallpaper, thinking it might peel off due to steam, try out some Wallies. These cut-out pieces of wallpaper come in assorted designs ranging from tiny to wall-sized. They install simply by moistening and setting in place and are easy to remove and reposition to suit your fancy. Choose designs from whimsical to pictures of nature online at www.wallies .com.

▲ Recessed lighting in a bathroom

If you are able to use existing plumbing for both the toilet and the tub, you'll find this remodeling job won't cost as much as you'd feared. Costs go up when you choose a bigger tub, if walls have to be moved, or if plumbing connections have to be changed. Medium-sized projects such as this one should stay in the medium-price range, especially since you aren't deciding to put the tub or toilet in a different place. You're simply replacing the current tub or toilet.

Make your bathroom seem bigger by using a visual trick. By applying a decorative mural of an outdoor scene to one wall, you can add depth to the room. I've found some picturesque ones in wallpaper books in paint stores and home improvement stores. One of my favorites is a mural of French doors that appear to open onto an outdoor garden. It's a lovely touch for a romantic bathroom. If you feel artistic, you can even paint one yourself. If you don't like the way it turns out or you later want a different look, just paint over it.

Another way to give a bathroom a lift is to raise the ceiling. I'm not suggesting you literally do that since that's a very expensive undertaking. Instead, why not try a faux paint treatment that will give the same effect? Try painting a lattice or molding design around the edge of the ceiling. I like to install actual crown molding and paint it the same color as the bathroom ceiling.

Lift the ceiling by painting faux clouds or stars. For a dramatic touch, paint the ceiling a dark shade of blue and then paint stars for a starry night effect. Or paint bands of color that graduate to lighter shades as they near the ceiling. It's a clever touch that fools the eye into thinking the ceiling is higher.

▶ A steam bath is a hot trend in luxurious bathrooms. It's possible to retrofit an existing tub or shower by adding vapor-proof doors. The generator, hidden away in a bathroom storage space such as a cabinet or closet, sends steam into the enclosure and voilà, steam. You can buy either a kit with everything you need or a steam bath module. The result is the next best thing to going to a spa.

A Complete Remodel

Even if you have the home of your dreams, it's likely there's something you want to improve in the bathroom. Have you always wanted a whirlpool tub? Or one of those fabulous showers with jets that splash you with warm, pulsing water? Sheer luxury. As much as you've sighed over those new, contemporary bathrooms in the model homes you've visited, you don't want to move. There are some things about your home that you don't particularly care for or they're outdated, but the good points of the house outweigh the bad.

But you walk into your bathroom one day and say, "This is it. I've had it." The tub is ugly and the problems with the toilet have made the plumber a too-frequent visitor to your house. You've tried all the tricks to put off a complete remodel until you have the time and money. The time is now. The bathroom and the kitchen are the two rooms that pay the biggest dividend when you remodel—now while you live in it and later when you sell your home. They're rooms where we spend a lot of time, and we want to enjoy every minute of it.

Big bath jobs require big skills. This is not likely to be a job to do yourself unless you have formal training in architecture or building contracting. If you're going to spend major dollars on this home improvement, I recommend strongly that you get professional planning and advice. Once I had a client who designed a very clever space that wrapped around one side of her house to enable her elderly parents to live with her. She had an architect look over her plan and make minor adjustments for electrical work and plumbing. Despite her good design, what she didn't know could have cost her extra money and time on the project if she had proceeded without professional advice.

Use your budget to plan. Budgeting has a connotation of saving money, but I feel it is really a plan for spending. No matter how large your budget for this remodel, you'll need to build in a cushion for elements you can't anticipate. There will be features you'll want to add that you won't know about until you're into the job. Perhaps you had thought you could just install some nice cabinets you saw in a home store. But the more you think about it, the more you realize you need custom cabinetry to get exactly the kind of wood, styling, and storage that you want. You want a whirlpool bath or a new shower enclosure—or both. Taking down a wall between the bath and the bedroom opens up space for a walk-in closet. Hmm, those custom closets are looking very appealing. Do you see how it is?

WHAT'S HOT

▶ Who wants to lie in a hard porcelain bathtub or stand under a trickle of water? (Not I!) Modern technology has found its way into the home bath. The Soft Bathtub features four layers of soft cushioning for a relaxing bath that becomes even more comfortable when the tub is filled with hot water. The BodySpa by Kohler offers a spa-style shower featuring a hydro-massage and a continuously heated waterfall. But beware: Both units come with hefty price tags.

▲ A beautiful spa bathroom

There are so many luxuries you can add to your bathroom remodel. What about a fireplace? A small sitting area? A plasma television you can watch from the tub? Gather every idea you come across that intrigues you and tuck examples away in your decorating file. You'll find yourself becoming more creative about what you want. By imagining so many possibilities, you can better decide on what's most important for you to have in your new space.

Fix Those Fixtures

New bath fixtures are sculptural and ultra-modern, luxurious decorative touches unlike the standard ones that were fine when bathrooms were just necessities. Faucets look like sculpture, sinks as if from an art exhibit, and tubs like something from a Roman bath. Whether these items are featured in a large bath or small, the luxuries in your master bath remodel will add comfort and **equity** to your home investment.

What are you looking for in a sink? Pedestal sinks used to be the norm in many bathrooms. They're updated now in beautiful columns of porcelain or glass. Or vessel sinks are used, sitting atop a pedestal of wood or stone. These sinks take up less floor space but add drama. The newest shapes in sinks include:

- A wall-mounted glass crescent
- A glass goblet shape that looks like a beautiful wine glass
- A cast-concrete sink that can be custom made
- A combination pedestal-cabinet
- A wall-mounted basin

ELSEWHERE ON THE WEB

▶ When you're ready to transform your bathroom into a spectacular, relaxing sanctuary with state-of-the-art fixtures, do some thorough shopping before you buy. To see exciting new shapes of sinks and tubs with various features, visit the Web sites of the major bath fixture manufacturers like Moen (www.moen.com), Waterworks (www.water works.com), and Kohler (www.kohler.com). Also see a slide show of distinctive sinks at www.bhg.com. You'll have a hard time deciding.

There are also multiple choices when it comes to tubs. For example, there are Victorian tubs and modern free-standing ones, whirlpools, traditional built-ins, specialty tubs, and special shapes. The Victorian bathtubs with claw feet used with a romantic decorating style don't just come in white anymore. You'll find a spectacular claw-foot bathtub in bold colors, even black. Tubs don't just seat one person anymore either. Many people are getting bigger tubs for a relaxing soak for two. There are tubs for everyone, from tubs for people who are bigger or taller to ones for people who want a deeper soak. Tub materials include acrylic, composite, marble, fiberglass, and the traditional porcelain over cast iron.

TOOLS YOU NEED

▶ Stores like Lowe's, Home Depot, Ace Hardware, and flooring manufacturers have handy calculators so you can figure out how much tile you need. Remember the rule: Always order at least 10 percent more than you think you'll need. There's nothing worse than running out of tile in the middle of a flooring project, only to find out you'll have to wait to get more—or not get it at all because it's been suddenly discontinued.

▲ A claw-foot tub

Maybe you're a shower person, not a bath person. Or you might choose a bath and shower combination. Look at the new showers in the model homes and if you're doing a major remodel, I think you'll want to include one. They are the height of luxury with their big floor plans and many jets. They also can be built with special lighting. Some feature a bench made of shower tile so you can sit and soap in comfort. Music can even be piped in.

All about Tile

The most appropriate flooring for bathrooms is tile or natural stone. It's waterproof and also provides a continuous surface when used on walls as well as floors. If you live in a climate in which such flooring material would feel cold during the winter, think about adding the luxury of radiant heat beneath them.

Visit a flooring store near you to find a wide variety of tile on the market today. Virtually every color is available either off-the-shelf or custom-made, and tile comes in sizes from one inch square to twenty-four inch square pieces. If you want your room to feel larger, choose a larger tile. For ease in cleaning, have the tile laid with small grout lines so dirt can't accumulate in them. Coordinate the color of the grout to match the tile, choosing as dark a color as you can to avoid white grout stains showing in no time.

Tile is the leading source of wall covering around a tub or a shower because of its waterproof nature. Coordinate the surround tile with a neutral, soothing color scheme in the floor and tub to create a more relaxing bath. If you want a dramatic look, tile is a perfect way to introduce color, shape, and texture. I've seen every color combination imaginable used. Clip ideas out of magazines to keep in your decorating file so you'll have a better idea of what you want when you go to the tile store.

Many people think you can't paint tile. I can tell you that you absolutely can. So if your tile from the 1980s is still in good condition but you can't stand the color, you can paint over it. First clean the tile thoroughly, including the grout. All traces of dirt, grease, and soap scum must be removed for the paint to adhere. There are products like calcium deposit removers that you can buy if you need them. Imperfections can be covered up by first sanding, then if needed coating with an enamel paint made just for this purpose.

Get Linked

People are especially interested in redecorating their bathrooms since the small space seems a small undertaking. I've got lots of information on bathrooms at the sites below.

FRESHEN UP YOUR BATHROOM WITH WEEKEND PROJECTS

Read about simple projects you can do in a weekend or day. With a little effort, you'll see a lot of change.
http://about.com/interiordec/bathweekend

MAKE YOUR SMALL BATHROOM SEEM LARGER

Many older homes have very small bathrooms. Find tips on ways to make your bathroom look and feel larger without knocking out walls.
http://about.com/interiordec/smallbath

BRING ELEGANCE AND LUXURY TO YOUR BATHROOM

By adding elegant, luxurious elements, you can create your own bath sanctuary.
http://about.com/interiordec/elegantbath

Chapter 10

The Kitchen: The Heart of the Home

Gather 'Round the Island

One of the biggest home trends I've tracked is how the kitchen is being reinvented. It's no longer your grandmother's kitchen—or even your mother's kitchen. It's not always bigger (although it often is). But it's more open and often connected to a family room or living room.

And the biggest change is that most new kitchens include a kitchen island. Yes, kitchen islands have been around for some time. But the new kitchen islands are bigger, shaped differently, and they're used for many purposes. The newest trend draws family and friends even further into the heart of our homes. Today while Mom or Dad cooks, the kids can have a snack at the kitchen island. I love parties in which guests gather around an island to help cook a meal or sit sipping a glass of wine as they watch the host or hostess cook.

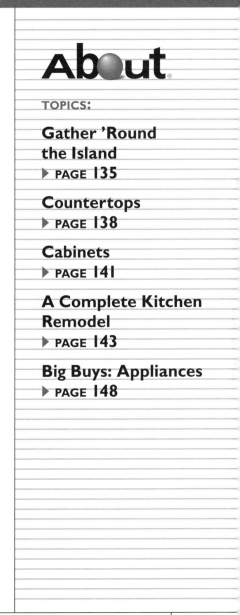

About.

▶ A custom-designed kitchen island can cost a fortune. Although installing a kitchen island is not a project for a beginner builder, if you're able to do the work yourself, you'll save money and you can customize it to your needs. With the right tools and patience, it's a project worth trying. Find helpful information and step-by-step directions at http://design. hgtv.com/kitchen on planning, designing, positioning, and building an island to fit into your space and budget.

▲ An island adds extra storage and workspace

Islands can expand your workspace and storage. People are working harder and when they come home to their kitchen, they expect it to work hard, too. The island must be a real workhorse, expanding the work area and helping with the ever-present storage issue. (Is there ever enough storage?) If you spend any time at all in your kitchen, try to fit in some kind of island, whether simple or elaborate.

One of the best uses for a kitchen island is to add seating to your kitchen. This is a good way to incorporate more family interaction into cooking and eating time. Why not extend the kitchen island so the kids can sit on barstools pulled up to the counter to do their homework while you cook? Two jobs get done at once and then dinner's served. Or extend a lowered countertop to serve as a table, placing chairs around it. I've seen wonderful islands that act as dividers between the kitchen and family room, with shelves at each end for books and family photos.

▲ Extra seating around a kitchen island

Islands come in many shapes and sizes. The old kitchen islands were rectangles or, occasionally in high-end homes, kidney-shaped islands. Today your island can be any shape you wish and as big as your kitchen can accommodate. Which shape will fit your kitchen best? If you have a long, narrow kitchen, the space will naturally dictate a long, narrow rectangle. But if the kitchen curves a little, why not try an island that curves as well? Are you a little taller (or shorter) than most people? Then make the island suit you in height as well.

ASK YOUR GUIDE

How can I have an island in my small rental home?

▶ Try one of the rolling worktables you can buy (or have someone handy make). Set on wheels so you can move them around your kitchen, they often come with steel, tile, or wood countertops. A bonus is that you can move it out of the kitchen into another room for ease in serving food. Even better, when you move you can take it with you for your new kitchen.

Choose an island that will make time spent in the kitchen easier. When I'm helping a client choose an island for her home, we sit down together and spend some time planning. What will be the function of the island? Does the new island have to serve multiple functions, such as food preparation, cooking, eating, entertaining, and dishwashing?

If you want to use the island for food preparation, you'll need plumbing. Including a stovetop, oven, or a warming drawer will require electricity. Some of the new islands have built-in deep fryers for the fried-food lovers in the family. Others feature a shelf for a microwave at a height for children to make popcorn and after-school snacks. Once you know the function you want the island to serve, you'll know what shape and size it should be. And if you're fortunate maybe you even have space for the ultimate luxury: multiple islands.

One of the best uses for a kitchen island is to add seating to your kitchen. This is a good way to incorporate more family interaction into cooking and eating time. Why not extend the kitchen island so the kids can sit on barstools pulled up to the counter to do their homework while you cook? Two jobs get done at once and then dinner's served. Or extend a lowered countertop to serve as a table, placing chairs around it. I've seen wonderful islands that act as dividers between the kitchen and family room, with shelves at each end for books and family photos.

Countertops

Especially exciting in kitchen design are the new countertop materials. I love the fact that even modestly priced kitchens can have terrific countertops that look like high-end materials. Although granite is now the number one choice of homeowners for their kitchens, there are lots of other choices out there. Here's a list of available options:

▶ The area between the stove, sink, and refrigerator is called the work triangle. Try not to interrupt the space needed for efficient movement from appliances to the work center. The walkway between your kitchen island and your stationary cabinets should be about 36" to 42" wide. The lower range (36") is enough if the island is near a bare wall. But if you are locating the island near a stove, refrigerator, or dishwasher, you'll need 42" or more between the island and the appliances for clearance and safety.

- **Granite:** Granite is elegant, holds up to heat, and comes in beautiful colors. Unfortunately it's also expensive and high-maintenance.
- **Engineered stone:** This material is composed of quartz particles. The upside is that it comes in more colors than granite, it has a scratch-resistant, nonporous surface, and maintenance is easy. The downside? It can be quite pricey.
- **Solid-surface:** This comes in many colors and patterns and is both seamless and stain-resistant. It's only moderately expensive, but hot pans and stains can damage the surface.
- **Ceramic tile:** The good thing about a tiled countertop is that you can install it yourself. It's also inexpensive, durable, easy to clean, and it handles hot pans without a problem. Tile comes in a wide selection of colors, patterns, and shapes. Unfortunately, tile can chip or crack, grout lines can become discolored and stained, and the countertop surface can be uneven.
- **Laminates:** These provide a smooth, easy-to-clean surface at a low cost. Many colors are available, and laminates are durable and easy to maintain. The downside? Scratches and chips are almost impossible to repair, seams show, and finishing and front edge choices can be pricey.
- **Wood or butcher-block:** This is a beautiful, warm countertop surface. It's smooth, easy to clean, and can be sanded and resealed when needed. The downside is that it can burn from hot pans, it holds dirt and mold, and needs to be resealed regularly.
- **Stainless steel counters:** These counters have a contemporary, industrial look. They're also heat resistant, easy to clean, durable, and seamless. They must be custom-made, so they're expensive. Other negatives are that stainless steel is noisy and may dent.

ELSEWHERE ON THE WEB

▶ It's a good idea to ask friends about their kitchen remodeling to determine how they like their choice of kitchen countertops. Some people like the look of granite but prefer the convenience of solid-surface, the clean lines of concrete, and the versatility of ceramic tile. For more information and opinions on the pros and cons of countertop surfaces, visit www.ehow.com and search for "kitchen counter-top tips."

▶ If your kitchen cabinets are relatively plain, you can make them more special with molding. Cutting the molding is easy with inexpensive tools available at home improvement stores. Build frames by applying molding to the doors with wood glue and finishing nails. Stain or paint the molding to match your cabinets. You'll have a new look for very little money.

- **Soapstone:** This is often used in historic homes but also popular in contemporary homes as a countertop and sink material. Soapstone, which comes in rich, deep colors, is smooth and somewhat stain-resistant. Unfortunately, it requires regular maintenance through applications of mineral oil. It may also darken and crack over time.
- **Marble:** This is very pricey so it's not often seen in kitchens. Use for an island or inset at a baking center. The upside: It's beautiful, waterproof, and heatproof. The downside: It's porous, it stains easily unless professionally sealed, and can scratch.
- **Concrete:** This is a new and unusual surface for the kitchen that's ideal for countertops in unusual shapes. It's heat- and scratch-resistant, can be color-tinted, and can be made in any configuration. The negatives are a mid- to high-range cost (because it's custom-made), it may crack, it looks industrial, and must be sealed because it's porous.

For the very latest in designer choices, don't visit your home center. Once items are available for the mass market, they're already on the way out for designers. If you want the hottest and newest products, watch television shows like HGTV's *I Want That* and look at design magazines to see what's coming next.

Sometimes you can revive a tired-looking kitchen just by installing new countertops. When you weigh the price of new cabinets against what countertops cost, you'll see that countertops can offer a relatively inexpensive way to redecorate your kitchen and a way to avoid the time, money, and hassle of a major kitchen remodel. Think of the last impressive kitchen you saw and, chances are, the countertops were what you noticed.

Cabinets

Cabinets, whether wood or laminate, big or small, are a mainstay of kitchens and not just for storage. They're the basis for organizing and streamlining your kitchen and making it function for you. Today's cabinets look to the past for inspiration, such as glass-fronted cabinets to show off beautiful dishes.

Wood cabinets are more popular than ever. Maple and oak are traditional choices that look good in any kitchen. The South American dark-grained woods lend an exotic look to modern kitchens. Laminate cabinets, an inexpensive choice used frequently over the past few decades, are still around but with newer, better-looking surfaces.

Not in a good position to rip out those old cabinets quite yet? Don't worry. I often find that putting in a new countertop so revitalizes a kitchen that new cabinets aren't necessary. Perhaps the old cabinets aren't outdated or ugly. Maybe they just need a good cleaning. Many a good wood has been found hiding beneath layers of grime built up from cooking. Thoroughly sponge with warm, soapy water, wipe with a clean, damp cloth, and then rub the wood dry. Bet they look better already.

Painting cabinets can complete your new look. If cleaning up the cabinets wasn't enough, take it to the next step with little effort. If the cabinets would look better in a different color, why not paint them? Even if they're laminate rather than wood, painting can give them a new look. Just ask the paint expert at a hardware or home improvement store for the particular kind of paint to use. Krylon makes a number of paints that adhere to a wide variety of surfaces, even to plastic.

Do opt for a paint that can be wiped clean, which is necessary in a kitchen. There are always fingerprints, cooking splatters, and an accumulated greasy film. Determining the color is almost more work than the actual painting since the selection is so extensive these days. Love a French country kitchen? Try painting a pale yellow on your top cabinets and a French blue on the bottom ones. Put up some simple café curtains of toile or floral material. You'll have an instant decorator look for very little money.

Love contemporary kitchens? If your kitchen cabinets are free of carving and froufrou touches, paint them a flat dark color such as slate gray. Black or red cabinets can be stunning in the right kitchen. Then balance the room with accessories of the same color.

Another way to freshen up cabinets is with new hardware. Every woman knows that no outfit is complete without the special sparkle jewelry conveys. You can add such sparkle to old kitchen cabinets with new cabinet hardware.

It used to be that there were only a few types of cabinet pulls—basic round knobs and rectangular handles. Their finishes came in just a few basic colors, usually the same color as the cabinet, and their materials were wood or metal. Now there are dozens of colors, many different types of materials, and thousands of places to find cabinet pulls. With a click of the mouse you can go on the Internet to find knobs and handles galore in a wide price range

Do you love a nautical theme? There are sculpted pulls of mermaids, lighthouses, ships, and other symbols of the sea. Flower lover? There are metal knobs with sunflowers, daisies, and roses. My daughter alternated cabinet and drawer pulls around the kitchen of small knives, forks, and spoons. I like coordinating cabinet hardware with wallpaper motifs like fruits and vegetables. If you have a vintage or country kitchen, you might like clear glass or old-fashioned porcelain knobs. Sleek metal bar handles can enhance the contemporary style of any kitchen. Try buying a single knob or handle if you're unsure of it and order the rest later if you like the difference

WHAT'S HOT

▶ There are so many kinds of kitchen cabinet hardware, you could spend days driving from store to store. Or you can look at kitchen cabinet hardware Web sites from the comfort of your home. Visit http://about.com/interiordec/cabinethardware. Narrow your choices by printing out your favorites before you visit stores. Then bring a sample home to try out in your kitchen.

it makes. You may find that adding new cabinet hardware eliminates the need for a more extensive renovation.

Here are some Web sites that feature unusual hardware choices:

- **HomePortfolio.com:** Offers more than 1,000 cabinet hardware designs.
- **AtlasHomewares.com:** Check out their selection of sea-themed cabinet hardware.
- **CapeCodBrass.com:** Features lines including Anne at Home, Baldwin Brass, and Schlage.
- **ProvidenceArtworks.com:** Browse their site by collection, some of which are made of bronze as well as river rocks.
- **RestorationHardware.com:** Hardware from reproductions to the latest contemporary knobs and handles.

A Complete Kitchen Remodel

Are you ready for a big kitchen remodel? If you've long struggled with an outdated or inconvenient kitchen, I can promise you that a major kitchen transformation will change your attitude toward meal preparation for years to come. Even people who love to cook or who have unlimited time (I don't know any, do you?) can lose interest cooking in a kitchen that doesn't meet their needs. Too little counter space is the biggest complaint, followed by outdated or nonworking appliances, and cabinets that are too high for a woman of average height.

This is a good time to draw up a budget. New kitchen cabinets will account for nearly half the total cost of your kitchen remodeling project. Though this might seem like a lot, think of the functionality and aesthetic value you gain from good kitchen cabinets. Stylish new cabinets entirely transform the look of a kitchen.

TOOLS YOU NEED

▶ When you've finally decided on a major remodel, expect to be without a working kitchen for as long as six months. I know that's a long time, but it is important to be ready for the long haul. You'll need to set up a temporary kitchen away from the construction zone, near a sink so you can go on with your life. Include a table and chairs, microwave oven, coffee maker, electric cooktop, mini refrigerator, and toaster oven.

Quality is a must since the cabinets will be opened and closed countless times over the years. Selecting a timeless style is crucial. Careful planning and researching all the options will pay off.

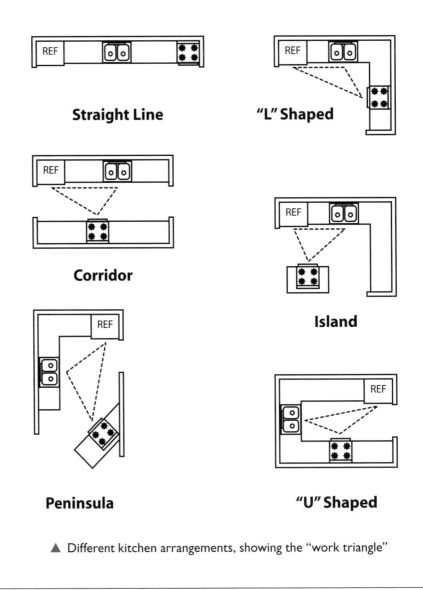

Straight Line

"L" Shaped

Corridor

Island

Peninsula

"U" Shaped

▲ Different kitchen arrangements, showing the "work triangle"

Take some preliminary measurements before you shop, since most cabinetry pricing is estimated by a running-foot measurement of your kitchen. Even if you're going to do the installation yourself, you should call in a professional at some point in the process to make sure you're doing everything correctly.

There are three choices in kitchen cabinets: stock cabinets, semicustom, and custom. Stock cabinets in standard shapes and sizes are, of course, the least expensive and are available at home improvement and contractor warehouse stores. Since they come in limited styles and sizes, they might not meet your needs, particularly if you have an unusually shaped kitchen. I tell clients that shopping for ready-made cabinets to fit in your space is like looking for a dress that's one size on top and another on the bottom.

Semicustom cabinets are built at the factory in standard sizes but offer more options in storage, design, and style. These might work if you need cabinets to fit in an awkward space. Look for extra features such as pullout shelves for pans, a lazy Susan, vertical dividers for trays and cookie sheets, wine racks, even a clever little appliance garage.

Custom cabinets are not for everyone, particularly if you're on a tight budget. Some people prefer to spend extra money on a better countertop, for instance, or better appliances. Standard or semicustom cabinets might serve your needs just fine. Even if this is your dream kitchen and you plan on living with it for a long time, other expenses of your home might preclude buying custom cabinets. If you are able to afford them, however, custom cabinets can give you the look you want.

Reconsideration is worthwhile. When you're examining all your options, reconsidering how you want your kitchen cabinets lined up on the walls is a good idea. As I mentioned earlier, a common

WHAT'S HOT

▶ Who wants to slave away in the kitchen while the rest of the family is enjoying themselves in the living or family room? Think about taking down a nonload-bearing wall and open up the space between these rooms. It's such a hot trend these days. If you can't take down the wall, perhaps you can cut out a space and create a pass-through bar, adding barstools on the other side to make the area more user-friendly.

complaint is that upper cabinets are often placed too high for the average woman. Constantly pulling out a step stool can be a hassle.

Many new or renovated kitchens have made room for a pantry cabinet with multiple shelves extending from floor to ceiling. I find that a big cabinet fits in about the same space as a refrigerator. If the refrigerator stands out conspicuously in an awkward place, replace with a cabinet with shelves for dishes, glassware, and **flatware** and move the refrigerator out of sight. Or place the cabinet next to the refrigerator for efficiency.

Think about what you'll store in the cabinets and where items will be most conveniently located for you and members of your family. Can your elementary school student get her cereal from the cabinet on her own and so make your life easier in the mornings? Sometimes I suggest that clients cut out wrapping paper or use poster board to help them envision where to place new kitchen cabinets. Just because a kitchen has looked a certain way in the past doesn't mean it has to stay that way now. It's your kitchen: Make it convenient and attractive for you.

It's an important debate: drawers versus cabinets. Who says you have to have a cabinet below the counter? Why not drawers? Increasingly new kitchens are featuring drawers for dishes, pots, pans, and other stored items. It makes sense because drawers are easier to access than reaching down to cabinets. The Europeans have been using drawers for years, and now the trend has moved across the Atlantic.

The kitchen sink is a pivotal piece in your kitchen. The same companies that brought you those beautiful bathroom sinks that have revolutionized decorating in that room have created stylish sinks for the kitchen as well. They're sleeker, deeper, even made to fit under the countertop instead of resting upon it. Some are throwbacks to farmhouse or apron sinks with deep lips and a homey style. They've become more than a functional place to rinse your hands or put a dish to soak: They're fashion now.

While I don't recommend making a fashion statement in, say, a red kitchen sink (though I've seen it done), there are no rules to incorporating the new sinks. So start clipping magazine and catalog pictures and visit home improvement stores to get ideas for your decorating file. There's more out there than that plain white or stainless steel sink.

Finish off your new sink or make an old one look better with a new faucet. There's nothing like a sparkling faucet, especially one of the new sculptural ones, to make a kitchen look fresh, even if that's all you're replacing. Take a look at the Web sites of leading sink manufacturers like Kohler or Moen and the home improvement stores to get more ideas for your kitchen. There are faucets for all types of kitchens. Although a faucet with a high neck and detachable spray for rinsing dishes, like that from a restaurant kitchen, is not for everyone, it might be perfect if you're planning an industrial kitchen with lots of stainless steel.

Do you like to accessorize the kitchen? I love the look of a kitchen that's uncluttered and clean and try to encourage my clients to keep counters and tabletops as clear as possible. There are always items that end up on the counters, but I think that everything in a kitchen (and elsewhere in the home, for that matter) should have a place out of sight. You, however, might love the new toasters, mixers, and coffee makers in designer hues, using them as the finishing touch in your kitchen.

With less appliance clutter, however, you might have room for a pretty wicker tray with a pot of flowers or an interesting small lamp to tuck in a corner for atmosphere. You could even line up a

WHAT'S HOT

▶ High-end appliances have now expanded from refrigerators to cover almost every appliance you could want for your kitchen. Instead of purchasing appliances in stock colors or finishes, think about having custom-wood panels made for the fronts of your new appliances to match kitchen cabinetry. That way appliances become part of the woodwork and end up looking like fine furniture. Most new appliances come with this custom option for door fronts.

row of family pictures along the wall above the counter. You'll have to decide how to decorate your kitchen space to suit your taste, needs, and interests.

Big Buys: Appliances

After kitchen cabinets, new appliances take the biggest bite out of your redecorating budget. Sometimes all you have to do is replace a dishwasher or perhaps a range. But often when people do a remodel, installing all new appliances is the rule. I've found that it's too hard to replace one or two appliances and coordinate these with existing appliances unless you go for white. Even stainless steel appliances can vary somewhat from year to year and manufacturer to manufacturer. It's likely that if one appliance is on its last legs, others bought at the same time will be too. Recently I drove through a subdivision near my home and spotted a number of major appliances left out for garbage pickup. All the homes had been built about twenty years earlier. You'd be fortunate to find a refrigerator or stove that will last twenty years these days.

Get ready to spend some serious money. Depending on how many appliances you're buying, you could be looking at spending several thousand to tens of thousands of dollars. These include the refrigerator/freezer, range and microwave, and dishwasher. While this part of your remodel is a big expense and takes a lot of time to plan and comparison shop, the difference these new additions will make to your kitchen will leave you in awe, as my clients have found.

Just as with cabinets, you probably shouldn't buy the same type of kitchen appliances as your old ones. Why not try something different, like the stainless steel that's become so popular? You don't have to stick with basic white or almond any more

ELSEWHERE ON THE WEB

▶ One of the aims of new appliance design is to save energy. Refrigerators use more energy than any other kitchen appliance, so they are a target for restyling and product development. Energy Star–qualified refrigerator models use at least 15 percent less energy than other models on the market today. For more information on energy-saving refrigerators, visit the Energy Star Web site at www.energystar.gov/index.cfm?c=refrig.pr_refrigerators.

(unless these are your preference). Again, as with kitchen cabinets, you can buy basic models or spend much more, depending on your budget.

Looking for a reason to buy new? The good thing about buying new appliances is their improved technology, as product specialists keep turning out innovations. Refrigerators have movable shelves and temperature-controlled sections that keep food fresher and safer. Even in-door water and ice dispensers have been improved. Microwaves can scan product bar codes and input instructions on how long to cook food. Dishwashers come in drawers so you can wash a few dishes and not wait until you have a full load. Each year appliances are becoming more energy-efficient, so you'll feel better about buying new when you see your electric bill.

Although refrigerators are one of the biggest expenditures in the appliance budget, they do last a long time. That's why it's important to buy exactly the one you and your family need. Your space, needs, and budget will determine whether you buy a regular-sized refrigerator or a big side-by-side refrigerator/freezer. Since the refrigerator is such a large fixture, choose a finish that will enhance your overall kitchen design.

One manufacturer has introduced a refrigerator with a clear glass front so that you can see exactly what's inside. Some people like this look, which is similar to ones used in grocery stores. By seeing inside the refrigerator without opening the door, you save on energy required. Another model of refrigerator has a television screen on the front door so you don't miss a moment of your favorite TV show while you're in the kitchen. You can also choose a refrigerator with a fingerprint-proof surface.

Refrigerated drawers or mini refrigerators can be installed in a kitchen island or pantry where food is prepared to save unneeded

WHAT'S HOT

▶ With a major kitchen remodeling, many people are investing a lot of money to install top-of-the-line industrial appliances. Whether you're a pastry chef, party planner, or gourmet cook, the sleek lines, touch controls, and durability of appliances are sure to inspire you. See the latest innovations in cooktops, refrigeration, and convenience offered by Dacor, Gaggenau, Jenn-Aire, Meile, and Viking in kitchen design stores and decide what you can't live without.

steps around the room. Like warming drawers, these refrigerator drawers are pricey additions to the kitchen but might be worth the expenditure for you.

Ranges have come a long way, too. Self-cleaning ovens, once a luxury option, are standard these days. Range innovations include vents that disappear and timers that make cooking no effort. (Almost.) There are also dual fuel stoves so you don't have to choose between gas and electric.

Once professional ranges were just for the professionals. Now you're as likely to see them in your neighbor's kitchen as in restaurants. I advise homeowners to buy the range they need, not to compete with the Jones family next door. While every dollar you spend on kitchens and bathrooms is returned when you sell your home, you don't want to get into debt over a professional range that you may not even use much.

What you likely will use is one of the new microwaves. As noted, some of them can read product bar codes and program themselves to cook any prepackaged product to the perfect temperature. This can result not only in better-cooked food but actually help those family members who have trouble seeing small print (or who don't read that well yet) to prepare their own meals. Even though most people install a microwave oven over the range these days, think about putting it within reach of your smallest child who is old enough to use it safely. Some open on both sides, making them ideal for sitting on a counter between the kitchen and family room.

Get Linked

Kitchens truly have become the heart of the home for many families. You'll find more information on kitchen design on my Interior Decorating site on About.com.

KITCHEN ISLANDS GO FRONT AND CENTER

Whether you have room for a large room-dividing island or a small table on wheels, a kitchen island is both functional and attractive. See photos of different kitchen islands and read how to make the most of what an island can do for you.

↗ http://about.com/interiordec/kitchenislands

GETTING STARTED ON A KITCHEN REMODELING PROJECT

From cabinets to appliances, flooring to lighting, you'll find helpful guidelines on starting your kitchen remodeling project.

↗ http://about.com/interiordec/startkitchen

WHAT TO CONSIDER BEFORE A KITCHEN REMODEL

Read some tips on planning, designing, and budgeting your new kitchen.

↗ http://about.com/interiordec/beforeremodel

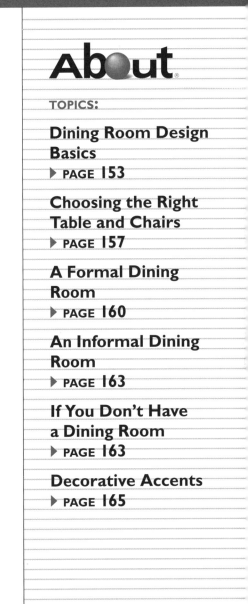

Chapter 11

Dining Rooms and Eat-In Spaces

Dining Room Design Basics

Have you heard the news? Dining rooms are back! Many people abandoned the dining room years ago to focus on watching television in the living room. They ate dinner from tables drawn up to sofas where they sat, as the boom in TV dinners began. But increasingly people are building dining rooms in their new homes or looking to buy homes with dining rooms. There's more entertaining at home as families large and small gather, and there's a return to dinner parties with friends. People are interested in nesting more. They're enjoying the homes they work so hard to have, and they want to dine and entertain there. The kitchen is the heart of the home, but the dining room is so often the place where we take time to dine in leisurely fashion and savor our time with family and friends.

About

▶ Decorate a table that's not in the best condition with a beautiful tablecloth. I've found them in all shapes, sizes, and colors from high-end decorating stores to flea markets and yard sales. Quilts are wonderful on tables in a country-style dining room. Old quilts can be cut up for placemats or for chair covers. Bamboo mats add a clean, stylish look to Asian or contemporary decorating schemes.

Do you use your dining room a lot? Or do you want to redecorate it so you can begin having family meals there, perhaps entertain friends and family? Maybe even host a big holiday dinner? Are you changing just a few things about the room, or are you doing a complete redecorating? Will that old dining room set and outdated china cabinet be going out the door? What about the window coverings? And that light fixture over the table. Is it going or staying?

The typical dining room is about the size of a small bedroom, large enough for a table and chairs but not much more. Even older homes have a dining room that will accommodate a nice family dinner. But new homes are being built with larger spaces that can combine dining with other activities.

There are a few basic components to a dining room. The most obvious is a table and chairs. You're going to be serving food in this room, and your family and guests need a place to sit and eat it. There are various options as to size, style, and materials when it comes to tables and chairs, which you'll read more about in the next section.

You may also want some storage in your dining room, such as a china cabinet to display lovely china and collectibles or a **buffet** or **sideboard** for serving dishes at those big holiday dinners.

Most china cabinets come with glass-fronted cabinet doors and have shelves for display. They're ideal for those lovely items you received for wedding presents such as china, silver serving pieces, and platters. China cabinets serve both a storage and a decorative function. The buffet or sideboard is also a place to display candlesticks or a silver tea service. In a more casual setting you can set a painting or family pictures on top.

Use the drawers of the china cabinet or the buffet to store items such as placemats and napkins for easy access when you dine. They can lie wrinkle free in the drawers until you're ready to use them. Using fine linen for dining adds a touch of elegance to a meal. If you have a set of silverware, store it in a special box in your china cabinet or buffet designed to prevent tarnishing. Drawers can also hold tablecloths and trays.

A chest of drawers also works for storage and style in the dining room. It can be tall and narrow or short and wide. Put plants, photos, and baskets atop it and use it like a buffet for storage. A chest of drawers is smaller than most buffets, so it will fit in a smaller dining room. It can even be used in another room later if you wish.

Color is another important part of your dining room redesign. Did you know the color red stimulates the appetite? I'm finding that many people are losing their fear of color, and one of the places where they are using it is in the dining room. Red is dramatic, although not for everyone. But once you've seen it on the walls of your dining room, I think you'll be very pleased. (And if you're not, it's a quick, easy fix to just paint over it.)

If a clear red is too much for you on all four walls, try it on a focal wall. Or try a darker red, a burgundy, or a juicy pomegranate for a rich accent. The dark wood of classic dining room furniture looks stunning against red hues.

We make a connection between other colors and food, too, like a dark, rich chocolate brown. What colors make you feel interested in being in the dining room to eat a meal and enjoy the time you spend there? Pull out those paint chips from your decorating file, and they'll give you some idea about food and color connections. There's celery green, biscotti beige, summer blueberry—the list is endless.

One of the best ways to introduce color in your dining room is with an area rug. Traditional dining rooms often feature a classic Persian rug with reds and other strong colors. Such rugs are not

▶ When you're ready to go shopping for a dining room set or individual pieces, be sure to take the floor plan and measurements of the room with you. What might seem like a perfect set in the furniture store might not fit in your space at all. If you try to fit in too many pieces, the room will be cramped. If you choose pieces that are too small, the room will feel cold and empty.

only rich and warm, but their intricate patterns can help to hide the crumbs associated with having family or a group of friends over to dine. You don't have to have a Persian rug, of course, if it doesn't appeal to you. Try an area rug that coordinates with or enhances your decorating style, like a bold geometric pattern for a contemporary dining room or a bright floral for an informal one. Be sure the rug is large enough to ground the table and chairs.

You may also want to introduce a theme or at least some art and decoration into your new dining room. I like to use art to create a feast for the senses in this room. Put your landscape painting in another room, unless it's a scene of a wheat field or something else associated with food. The dining room can be a perfect place to hang lush still lifes with fruit or vegetables, such as an oil painting of luscious peaches or a bowl of green pears. Or try a grouping of paintings of vegetables such as asparagus, artichokes, or eggplants in attractive gold frames over the buffet. The artists of a couple of hundred years ago knew what they were doing when they painted images of the bounty of the earth. This type of art stimulates an appreciation for food and makes you eager to taste what you've cooked for your meal.

If you're not into the food theme, consider creating a wonderful Asian-themed dining room. This is an especially good theme if you have a fast-paced life. Imagine how calm you'll feel when you sit at your dining room table surrounded by the cool, elegant design of an Asian dining room. To create the look, try some simple black Asian furniture, which you can buy new or used or paint some pieces you already own. Put some striking china and Asian decorative pieces in the china cabinet and on the top of the buffet. Woven mats in cool colors like green or blue will look good on the dining room table. Continue the natural fiber look by putting bamboo blinds up or simple drapery panels at the windows.

If yours is a country-style dining room, hang some colorful dishes on the wall behind the buffet. Or place them on plate stands in the china cabinet so they can be seen. If you've put a quilt on your dining room table as a tablecloth and have other quilts that you don't use much, think about cutting one up and framing the pieces on a wall. They're wonderful wall art. Other art can include botanical prints or panels of floral fabric stapled to artist's canvas or simply framed and placed on the wall.

Scenes of harvests and of tables laden with the bounty of the fields fit well in a country-style dining room, as do any rural scenes of the country that evoke the serene, comforting feel of fields and winding roads.

A Tuscan or French country decorating scheme is a popular style for dining rooms. Who wouldn't want to walk into a room that reminded them of Tuscany or France, two places associated with wonderful food just steps from your kitchen? Paint the walls in warm, earthy colors. Try one of the special Venetian plaster treatments discussed in Chapter 6. Create a French country look with different fabrics on your table and windows along with antique furniture (or at least old furniture), and you'll feel like you're transported to another country whenever you eat in your dining room. I think if you try either of these decorating schemes, you'll be eating in the dining room more often.

Choosing the Right Table and Chairs

The dining room is an important room to plan properly. If you think about it, you want comfort in this room as much as in your living room or bedroom. Perhaps you think you don't spend much time in this room. After all, how long does anyone sit at a table and eat?

But reflect for a moment. Remember the last time you had family or a group of friends over for dinner? No one just ate quickly

ELSEWHERE ON THE WEB

▶ Not everyone can afford original oil paintings to decorate their home. Not to worry! There are lots of Web sites that offer a wide range of art, framed or unframed, at reasonable prices. ArtSelect (www.artselect.com), Art MegaShop (www.artmega shop.com), and The Guild (www.guild.com) are just a few of the online resources of fine art for decorating. You can choose from different themes, media, artist, and style to get just what you want.

and got up, did they? I'll bet they lingered for quite a while over the last cup of coffee.

No matter the style of dining room you decide to create, you will need to plan on finding the right size table for your room and enough chairs for the kinds of gatherings you will have. Don't forget to bring your decorating file when you shop.

When working on the dining room, it's important to plan for comfort. No one wants to bump elbows while dining. If kids wind up bumping elbows, that's likely to cause embarrassing spills, which is aggravation you don't need. I advise clients to allow about twenty-four to thirty inches between each person, if the room allows it. That's ideal for well-being. It's also helpful for there to be about two and a half feet across the table, too, so you don't feel you're eating off a bench. Dining room tables have a standard height of about thirty inches.

While you're planning for that distance between diners at your table, check that the placement of table legs isn't in anyone's way when seated. Push at the table to make sure it doesn't feel flimsy or wobbly. What about the chairs? Are they comfortable? Whether you have children or not, take care that the fabric on the seat cushions is protected against stains. After all, even the most careful diners sometimes drop food in their laps and onto the chair seat when they get up.

What shape do you like for your table? It may be that the shape of the room determines this for you. If the room is small and square, a round table may be best. And a long narrow room seems to beg for a long narrow table. There are square tables, even tables shaped like an octagon. If you haven't ever bought a table for the dining room, you might find it helpful to tape off a shape on the floor to see whether there's room around

▶ It's so easy to find inexpensive decorative pieces in an ethnic or foreign style. Discount home goods stores are almost everywhere, and there are thousands of Web sites. Without spending a lot of money, you can find authentic and stylish decorative plates, bowls, serving pieces, pictures, mirrors, and artificial floral arrangements to enhance almost any style of room. I love to visit such stores often to not miss out on new shipments.

it. No one wants to feel squeezed by too big of a table for the room.

If the room is small, I like to make a room seem bigger by creating a table from a piece of glass placed on top of a pedestal. The pedestal can be a stone column, a big ornamental jar, or just about anything that will support a glass top and look good in your room.

Some dining room tables have extension leaves that can be inserted to expand its size when needed. There are drop leaf tables with sides that can be lifted up and secured if necessary. I've even seen tables suspended by cables that could be lowered from the ceiling for use and raised out of sight when not being used.

Of course, you need chairs to go with that table. The first decision to make is how many chairs you need. You don't need enough chairs for a big dinner party, since you can pull extra side chairs in from other rooms for entertaining. However, you do want enough for the size of your immediate family—usually four to six.

Whether you're buying dining room chairs as part of a set or by themselves to go with a table you already have, there is such a large variety you might have trouble narrowing down your choice. Do you want chairs with arms or without? People have very definite opinions on this. Some people want to rest their arms after they dine but have been cautioned too many times by their mothers not to put their elbows on the table. Remember, though, that if you're trying to get a number of people around a table, armchairs take up a little more room and so allow fewer people at the table. If you have room, think about getting some extra chairs and placing them along a wall for extra seating later.

Just as you did with the table, check the legs on the chairs. They should be constructed in such a way that they don't get in your way as you sit down or get up from the table. Finally, make sure there is enough room between the bottom of the table and your lap. If the

ASK YOUR GUIDE

My dining room table doesn't seat very many people. What can I do to make it work for larger groups?

▶ Not everyone has a dining table large enough to seat family and friends. Use the table as a base and build a larger plywood top to fit over it for big gatherings. Depending on the size of your room, the top can be round or oval. For easy storage, cut the top in half down the middle and attach the pieces with heavy hinges. When you're finished, fold it in half and slide it under a bed or into the garage.

space is too snug, you won't be able to cross your legs and clothing could be snagged by a stray splinter.

Unless you have a very formal dining room, you don't have to match your chairs. Pairs of chairs in different styles and colors can look complementary around a dining room table. I've painted chairs different colors and used different materials on the seats for a charming casual setting. I've also used mismatched chairs, all painted the same color with matching seat covers. Varied slipcovers can be used for a fun creative touch, too. One furniture manufacturer makes a table with four differently colored upholstered chairs that's a popular seller.

Don't be afraid to try chair alternatives. If you have a square or rectangular table, on one side why not try a padded bench, either with a back or without, with chairs on the other side? Or use a bench on the long sides and chairs at each end. Benches work well in a casual dining room or nook. Kids love benches because they feel they're sitting at a picnic table. If the table is near a window, put chairs on the opposite side of the table facing out the window. Need storage? Consider installing a bench or window seat with a hinged, lift-up seat and use the storage space inside for seldom used or out-of-season items for the dining room or kitchen.

A Formal Dining Room

Many people like having a formal dining room for entertaining guests. It also makes the time you spend there seem very special. When you sit at a beautiful wood dining table laid with sparkling china, gaze upon a lovely color, decorative paint treatment, or wallpaper on the walls, and feel the coziness of sumptuous window treatments, you can't help but feel your senses are full. There is something very satisfying and familiar about a formal or traditional setting. Dining in a formal setting encourages us to be more cultivated, to slow down, and to savor. It provides a way to fully nurture ourselves and our guests.

▲ A formal dining room

As with formal design in a living room, there is balance and order in a formal dining room. The table is centered and chairs facing each other surround it. An arrangement of candles and decorative items is symmetrical. Sometimes strong colors like red or burgundy are used for drama and effect. Draperies are neat and orderly, neither fussy nor casual. There's an elegance about the room. More is not always better: The room may be elaborately furnished but not fussy. A formal dining room is often found in a home decorated uniformly in a formal style. When decorating a home, I feel it's best not to make one room (such as the dining room) formal and the rest of the house casual in style.

Certain colors and details evoke a formal look and feel.
Try painting the walls a rich dark color such as red, brown, or navy. For more depth, try painting stripes of the same color in a different finish, for example, combining satin with matte. Light striking such walls creates an understated elegance, a hallmark of a traditional style.

Next, hang a large mirror over the buffet. You can install electric or candle sconces on either side to reflect light around the room. Perhaps hang a formal piece of art such as a landscape. Place more candlesticks on either side of the buffet, remembering that traditional style calls for balanced arrangements of furniture and accessories. Then hang new draperies on the windows. They should be of a luxurious fabric such as silk or satin. The window treatment should be pleated or draped, which is a more formal look than that of simple tab curtains. Whether you choose plain or printed fabric doesn't matter, so long as the look is subtle and rich.

The dining room furniture should be matching and should also be constructed of a good quality hardwood. If your table is not the best quality but you don't want to replace it, cover it with a quality tablecloth to complement the draperies. If you have hardwood floors, place a luxurious rug such as a Persian or an Oriental beneath the table.

There should be an artfully arranged formal centerpiece of flowers. If the flowers aren't real, the highest caliber of silk is acceptable. Set the table with your best china, crystal, and silver, and set out lots more candles in elaborate holders.

ELSEWHERE ON THE WEB

▶ Love the shabby chic look? Rachel Ashwell's site (www .shabbychic.com) tells how to collect vintage linens or use a bath of tea to age linens, using them lavishly in your dining room. Make a window valance from beautifully embroidered antique handkerchiefs, tablecloths, or napkins, or drape a pretty tablecloth over a wooden rod. Layer several tablecloths on a table for a rich look. Be sure to put lots of flowers on the table with lacy napkins to complete the look.

An Informal Dining Room

Informal dining rooms are casual and comfortable. People who have small children especially favor them, as do those for whom the dining room is the primary place for eating. The style is characterized by informal furniture and a de-emphasis on symmetry in furnishings and decoration.

To create an informal dining room, paint the walls a light, airy yellow or green and hang simple tab-top curtains of cotton or linen on the windows. Or try bamboo or matchstick shades. If privacy isn't an issue, simply use a fabric valance at the top of the window. A buffet in a light rustic oak or rattan can store linens and allow a place for serving. A big china cabinet can hold collectibles like a tea set, china, and family photos in varied frames. Casual materials are also used on chair seat covers. Sometimes a bench is used on one side of the table, set across from nonmatching chairs. Cushions on informal dining room chairs used by children should be treated with a fabric-protection finish.

Table centerpieces might be a simple bunch of garden flowers or wildflowers filling a pitcher. Tablecloths are simple cotton and place mats woven or made of cotton. Tableware and glassware are casual, ranging from colorful pottery to white earthenware. Stainless steel flatware is a practical utensil. Choose a cotton or sea grass rug in a simple, contemporary pattern or cheerful floral print beneath the table.

If You Don't Have a Dining Room

If your home lacks a separate dining room, you can still create a pleasing dining area with its own identity. It's important to select furniture for such a setting, like in an eat-in kitchen, that blends in with the room. Or if you have a combination living room/dining area, don't mix a kitchen-style **dinette set** with classic living room hardwood furniture.

ELSEWHERE ON THE WEB

▶ Finding a casual dining set
to your liking is not always
easy, since furniture stores
often focus on impressive
investment pieces. Pier 1
Imports (www.pier1.com)
and Cost Plus World Market
(www.worldmarket.com)
offer casual, comfortable sets
that work well in a breakfast
room or in a corner of the
living room for snacking.

▲ An open kitchen with dining area

Breakfast nooks are not just for eating breakfast. They're
an inviting space for lunch, snacks, and casual dinners. Some people
prefer a cozy breakfast area to eating in a dining room, especially
one situated near a window overlooking a garden or the backyard.
By buying better furniture than an ordinary lightweight kitchen set
for an eat-in kitchen, you can make a special, conveniently located
dining area. Even the smallest spaces can usually accommodate a

bistro set. I once found a slate-topped table with wrought iron legs and four chairs that was perfect in an informal eat-in space. It stood up to the demands of a young family's mealtimes while adding style.

A new trend is to turn the dining room into a combination dining room and study or home office. For a part-study, add some good quality bookcases, a comfortable chair for reading (if space allows), and a display of collectibles. One of the nicest such settings I've done featured a big mahogany table bought from a closing local library branch. Men and women alike love the look and versatility this dual use provides.

Decorative Accents

Decorative accents in a dining room include lighting fixtures, lamps, candles, wall sconces, paintings, sculptures, and murals. Any one of these can inspire the style for the rest of the room as well as serve as colorful textural accents to complete a look. Sometimes you can find a spot in the dining room for a special item that doesn't fit in any other room.

I remember reading that legendary actress Marilyn Monroe always viewed her reflection critically in a full-length mirror before leaving home dressed for an important function. If one piece of jewelry she'd chosen to adorn her outfit seemed to attract too much attention, she would take it off. No one piece was allowed to dominate the total effect. That's an important fashion rule to adopt in our homes.

Placement is important. To prevent a dining room from appearing flat, in the sense of all on one level, take care that decorative accents vary in height. A pleasing nontraditional arrangement on a buffet features several candlesticks of varying heights on one

WHAT'S HOT

▶ Adorn your dining room light fixture with fancy braid or ribbon from a craft store. I once used those inexpensive sparkling mesh sleeves for decorating wine bottles to dress up plain shades for a client's holiday party. The effect of light shining through the fabric shade was striking.

▶ Select an appropriate size and style of chandelier for your dining room. On my Web site I have a helpful article called "Choosing the Right Size Chandelier." You need to consider the size of the room, the size of the table, and the height of the ceiling. Then install a dimmer control on the wall to vary the level of lighting.

end, making for a grouping of interest. For the same effect, group a big painting next to several smaller ones over a dining room buffet. Fine restaurants often group several mirrors to reflect shimmering candlelight or an attractive view. You can duplicate in your own home the effect of mirrors lining a small restaurant's walls, which adds light and space. People like to look at themselves as they eat, I've noticed. One Hollywood actress from the glamorous 1940s decorated her dining room with mirrored walls to replicate her favorite Parisian restaurant. The lovely ambiance of the room made it a popular site for entertaining.

Give considerable thought to choosing lighting for your dining room. In my view, nothing accentuates a room more than proper lighting. For the dining room that usually entails hanging a marvelous chandelier. Its purpose is to add a decorative element beyond its basic function of illuminating a room. A large lighting fixture makes more of a style statement than does a lamp. This can be a sparkling crystal or glass chandelier or a branching fixture with interesting bulbs, perhaps decked with little lampshades. I've seen chandeliers made of antlers for a rustic home and punched metal for a Southwestern home. Chandeliers with electric candles are a throwback to the use of real candles but safer and easier, since you won't have to scrape wax off the dining room table.

There's nothing more luxurious than a beautifully set table to influence the mood of your dining area. One of my clients still remembers the beautiful lace tablecloth that covered her grandmother's dining room table. A treasured family heirloom, it made the room especially elegant. Too fine to use during big family dinners, it was put back on the table after dishes were cleared. During mealtimes damask placemats and cloth napkins were used.

Today's table linens are just as fancy as those of bygone generations but easier to care for. You no longer have to remove the cloth during the meal or fret about getting it ironed in time for the next party. Fabrics have built-in finishes to make them wrinkle free and to prevent stains.

Your choice of table linens depends on whether you're aiming for a formal or informal look. For a formal look, set a fancy, luxurious tablecloth with crystal, china, and a candle centerpiece. Place raw linen place mats on your wood table for an informal look and add a small tray with chunky pottery votives and a vase of flowers for a casual family dinner.

Whether you have a square, oval, oblong, or round table, you can find the right size tablecloth ready-made in just about any department store or home goods store. Practical tablecloths come in standard sizes to fit most tables.

Square tablecloths are 52" x 52" and fit tables 28" x 28" to 40" x 40" that seat four people. Oval tablecloths are 60" x 84" and fit tables 36" x 60" to 48" x 72". Oval tables usually seat six to eight people. Oblong tablecloths are 52" x 60" and cover tables with dimensions of 28" x 46" to 40" x 58" that seat four to six people. Round tablecloths are 60" and fit tables with a diameter of 36" to 48". These tables seat four people. If your round table is 48" diameter to 58" diameter, you'll need a 70" tablecloth. Round tables of this size accommodate four to six people. Do you have a round table 66" to 78" diameter that seats four to six people? You'll need a 90" tablecloth.

Always select a tablecloth size that allows the cloth to hang at least 8" over the edge of the table all the way around. Though the color choice might not be exactly right, you're sure to find something that will work for everyday dining. Choose one that looks best in your dining room and with your china. Don't forget to buy coordinating napkins, too.

Try a quick sewing project for your table. It's easy to make a tablecloth for a round table. Choose material that is complementary to your design plan and that coordinates with the fabric on your dining room chairs and curtains. That doesn't mean it has to match. If yours is a formal dining room, find formal material such as velvet and satin; reserve cotton for an informal style.

A 90" table will require $5\frac{1}{8}$ yards of material that is 54" wide. After you fold the material into quarters, use a guide to cut the material in a circle by tying $1\frac{1}{2}$ yards (46") of ordinary string to a piece of chalk. Hold the string in place on a corner of the fold and use the chalk to draw a radius circle. Cut through the layers of material on the chalk line, and when you unfold the material you'll have a perfect circle. Hem the skirt, or if you're not handy with a needle or a sewing machine, apply iron-on hem fabric or tape. To sew on trim, you'll need about eight yards of material for a skirt.

Be ready for formal occasions. To create an elegant table to showcase your finest china, silver, and crystal for a holiday, there are beautiful tablecloths, napkins, and place mats in fine linen or silk in every color of the rainbow. During the Christmas holiday, I particularly love to use Christmas china and decorate the table with gold, silver, red, or green linens. If you need a particular pattern or a custom color, you might want to make your own tablecloth and napkins out of designer fabric.

You can make your dining area unique with a lovely centerpiece. Whether you use something simple or elaborate, bought or handmade, you'll set your table apart from others. If you love the look of the seashore, why not put a bowl of shells in the center of the table? A big wooden bowl of green apples adds charm to a country-style dining room, and the apples can be eaten during the week. I have a friend who treasures the clear Depression glass basket her mother passed down to her, which she fills alternately with fruit, shells, or flowers from her garden.

Anyone can set fresh flowers on the table these days, lending color and scent to the dining area. Even if you don't have a green thumb like my friend, you can pick up pretty, healthy blooms for a few dollars from the florist or local grocery store. One couple I know has a dozen red roses on the dining room table every day. It seems the husband brought home a dozen red roses for his new bride early in the marriage and has kept up the tradition for more than thirty years. You can imagine how heartwarming it is to step into such a room.

Flowers freshen a room and lend a lovely seasonal look. Buy a few pots of tulips or daffodils for a fresh breath of spring, a bunch of daisies or dahlias for summer, and spicy mums for fall.

And don't stop with a wreath on the front door at Christmas. Put a big potted poinsettia, red amaryllis, miniature Christmas tree, or evergreens surrounding candles as a centerpiece on the table for a festive touch. Use decorations that symbolize your family heritage when family and friends gather. Actually, it's a good idea to burn candles at the table often, not just on special occasions. They're the kind of touch that can make any mealtime special.

Get Linked

You'll find some information on decorating a dining room at my Interior Decorating site on About.com. The following links to dining room hints are helpful.

THE RIGHT SIZE CHANDELIER

Use the measurements here to help you choose the perfect chandelier for your dining room.

http://about.com/interiordec/chandelier

LEARN SIMPLE NAPKIN FOLDING

Follow the tutorials to learn decorative napkin folding. You'll be surprised at what a special touch a pretty napkin adds to the table.

http://about.com/interiordec/napkinfold

REMOVE WATER MARKS FROM WOOD FURNITURE

It's inevitable that your wood tabletop becomes marred after use. Learn how to remove the water marks left by sweating glasses and steamy dishes.

http://about.com/interiordec/watermarks

Chapter 12

Storage and Organization

Sorting It Out

Clutter: It's everywhere. We've been called a nation of pack rats because we seem to want to hold onto everything. Just take a look around your own space right now. If you're like most people, nearly every surface has something on it. There's a stack of mail lying here, a project left there, magazines and newspapers on the reading chair and stuffed in a basket beside it, collections overflowing a display cabinet, bookshelves crammed with books you can't let go of, way too much furniture in most rooms, and let's not even look in the garage!

   Clutter has become such a big problem that it has created a new occupation of professional organizers. You might think that professional organizers simply show up at someone's house and get rid of some things, put other things away—but it's not that simple. Because, after all, if it were that simple, the homeowner could have just done the job herself. I've found that the best professional organizers are those who have not only experience in

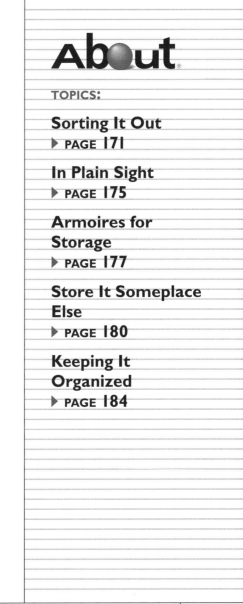

home decorating but knowledge of why people accumulate things and can't get rid of them.

Are you like so many Americans who find it difficult to get rid of things? If your home has become filled with clutter, you've probably told yourself that you should just be able to clean up and clear away. Maybe you've even given yourself a hard time about it. If you were a better person, you figure, you would be able to keep a neater house, even with your busy schedule. But as the days pass, you find the task just too big to tackle.

It's time to take another look at the problem. The clutter is there because so many of us are overwhelmed with our overly busy lives. We walk in the front door and find our homes a reflection of the multitasking, manic lives we're leading.

It's time to let go of too much stuff that's leaving you feeling like you have no control and no place to relax. Letting go of things that are just taking up space can be incredibly freeing, not to mention give you more room.

Forget the excuses. I can almost hear you saying that you're too busy, that you don't have time to get organized. However, it's been my experience that not getting organized in the first place is what is time-consuming. It's not just that it takes longer to find whatever you're looking for or that you make a trip to the store to buy a pair of pantyhose when, if things had been organized, you would have seen the two pairs you already have. I'm talking about the emotional toll that clutter takes on us. Even if some people can overlook the clutter around them, I think most of us find it really discouraging. We blame ourselves for not keeping our surroundings in better shape, for not managing our homes.

The trouble is that by the time we're finally fed up with the clutter, it's too big a job to tackle. And who has an entire weekend or more to take on the task? The more drained we feel, the worse clutter gets—until we're in a vicious circle. But you don't have to live with this situation. Clutter didn't accumulate in one day, so thinking we can get rid of it in one day is unrealistic. Instead, every day set a timer for half an hour, stay focused, and clear away as much as you can. Don't get bogged down looking at individual papers but box them to go through another time. Avoid sitting down and becoming sentimental about a particular item. Remember your goal of clearing the clutter and work until you hear the timer go off. Then resume your usual pursuits. If you follow this practice consistently, you soon will make a dent in the clutter.

Good advice remains true. You've heard the advice to get rid of items like unworn clothes so many times, you probably don't hear it anymore. But it bears repeating. So many of us hold onto so many things, particularly clothing, until they're so out of style that no one would want them. I've seen bell bottoms from forty years ago in the back of a client's bedroom closet when I was helping to organize the space. Yes, fashion trends do repeat, but do you think you'll actually want to wear such old items again? The same goes for clothes you plan to wear when you drop twenty pounds. If you haven't worn them in several years, better to pass them along to charity and when you do lose that weight, you can reward yourself with clothes that are more fashionable, perhaps even more stain- and wrinkle-resistant.

Before you throw out old items from a clutter sweep, take a moment to consider where best to donate them. Certain things may be more needed by a charity than others. Some facilities can only accept certain items or have limited storage. Also don't be afraid to ask a charity to which you're making a donation for a receipt for tax purposes—they expect this and some will give you one without asking. Finally, call ahead to make sure your charity of choice can accept your donation at a certain time. Volunteers

ELSEWHERE ON THE WEB

▶ Monica Ricci founded Catalyst Organizing Solutions in 1998 to help people organize and declutter their homes. By getting rid of unnecessary things, we can live our lives more fully and pleasurably. If you would like to read more about Ricci's philosophy of stuff, her ideas on time management, and how to hear one of her motivational speeches, visit her Web site at www.catalystorganizing .com.

might be scarce when you come by, and city ordinances prohibit boxes and bags sitting outside a charity after hours.

Ask friends and family to help declutter. We take friends with us when we shop to advise us on purchases. Think about asking a friend to help you if you have trouble letting go of things. I got this idea years ago when a friend stopped by while I was clearing out clutter. I had to keep working because everything was spread out in the living room, though I didn't want to miss visiting with my friend. So she fixed a cup of tea and sat down to watch. Before I knew it, she was offering advice on what I should keep and what I should discard. It was very helpful to have her insight.

Professional organizers do this for you. Unlike you, they aren't emotionally attached to your things and so are able to help you decide what to do with it. Unfortunately, not everyone can afford to hire a professional organizer or can work out a compatible schedule for an organizer to come to her house. So why not ask a friend to stand in for one? You might have fun while you get your clutter problem resolved.

It used to be that when people had cluttered homes, they kept it a secret, discouraging visits from friends and not letting their children invite friends for a sleepover. They certainly didn't advertise the fact that their homes looked like pack rats lived there.

But nowadays people are revealing their clutter problem out of desperation to change. They open their homes to television shows like *Clean Sweep*, *Clean House*, and *Mission: Organization*. There are countless articles on organizing and decluttering.

Everyone, it seems, is seeking another's "tough love" to pressure him into decluttering. There are even clutter support groups.

▶ Do some research from your computer. Major nation-wide charitable organizations maintain Web sites listing their locations in every community. Goodwill Industries (www.goodwill.org) provides training and jobs. The Salvation Army (www.salvation armyusa.org) collects donations to support other charitable organizations as well as disaster relief around the world. Area Junior League (www.ajli.org) women are committed to promoting voluntarism, developing the potential of women, and improving communities. These charities are reliable and contribute to local and world needs.

In Plain Sight

Clutter creates stress. When your environment is messy and disorganized, you can't help but feel even more hassled. No one likes to spend precious time looking for something buried. That's why it's so important to get control of your space. There are many ways to do this if you're willing to commit a little time to getting and staying organized.

Setting up shelving is one of my favorite tricks for decluttering. Shelving takes advantage of vertical space while providing a place to show off meaningful keepsakes. Open storage performs a double function.

Using simple shelving is one of the most basic methods of storage. Shelves can be bought in precut lengths or can be cut at a home improvement store. If the shelving is for an out-of-sight area like a closet, buy fiberboard or plywood. For higher-end shelves that will be publicly visible, buy good quality wood and stain or paint it.

First use a measuring tape to measure the space for the shelves. How much weight will the shelves hold? Unless they are only needed to support light objects, you should use screw anchors to prevent shelves from pulling away from a wall and crashing to the floor. If you intend to put especially heavy objects on shelves, use a stud finder so the shelves will be more securely anchored.

Metal shelving standards (long metal strips that hold brackets) used with arm brackets (which can be decorative) offer a good way to put up shelves quickly and easily. Look in the shelving section in home improvement stores for new products that allow you to adjust mounted shelves to whatever height is desired.

Shelves aren't the only open-storage method for getting organized. You can also use bookcases and furniture pieces

ELSEWHERE ON THE WEB

▶ Author Barbara Kavovit features a tip of the week on her Web site at www.barb arak.com. Recently, she listed instructions on how to build a shelf for storage. With her simple directions on using tools most homeowners have on hand (such as a tape measure, drill, level, and screwdriver), even someone who doesn't think she's handy should have no trouble putting up a shelf. And every success with a project builds confidence to take on another.

with glass fronts such as china cabinets, hutches, and cabinets. It's important to display attractive contents in these, of course. No one wants to view unappealing clutter. Mix books that have interesting spines with a few knickknacks (not too many!) and you combine making a decorating statement with solving a storage problem. Don't hide your pretty dishes or collectible plates in a dark cabinet. Display them in an open storage unit or hang them on a wall to show them off.

▲ Cabinets with glass fronts for attractive storage.

Show off your collectibles. Although it's fun to collect special items, if you're not careful you can end up with a serious storage problem—or a clutter problem. What kind of collection do you have? Can you use it as a design element in a particular room? If you have a collection of old typewriters, consider grouping them on shelves in your home office. Just don't feel you have to display all of them at one time if you have too many. Box excess ones to keep out dust and then put them in storage. A collection of perfume bottles would be lovely grouped on a mirrored tray on your vanity. I helped a client make the most of her lighthouse collection by grouping them in a hutch we found at a yard sale. She found herself going around the house gathering scattered lighthouses and nautical items until the guest bedroom that held the hutch collection began to look like a seaside bed and breakfast. This is now a space her friends love to visit.

Armoires for Storage

Not everything has to be within easy reach. Think about it. Sometimes we keep things around us that we look at so much, we don't really see them anymore. Do you have items that can be put away in hidden storage such as into an armoire, a chest of drawers, or cupboard, even under a bed? Christmas decorations don't have to sit in a closet using up valuable space if you have a garage, utility room, an attic, or a basement (providing there is no moisture issue). Move them into one of these rooms. Items such as ironing boards that are used only every week or two can be hung on the back of the door to the laundry room or a bedroom. Anytime you can use vertical storage—through space above furniture, beds, and counters—you've maximized your storage potential. Consider not only shelves and bookcases but armoires and other closed cabinets.

TOOLS YOU NEED

▶ Decorator TV shows are a good source of information on home organization. Learn more tips and tricks for sweeping out clutter, cleaning up, and organizing your home on the *Clean Sweep* Web site at http://tlc.discovery.com/fansites/cleansweep/cleansweep.html. You'll find important information about shows along with summaries of each episode, complete with before and after photos. Check out the index of helpful tips from each episode and learn how to get rid of all that extra stuff.

Armoires function as decorative storage solutions. I believe an armoire is one of the best forms of storage for every room in the house. Armoires, which are tall cabinets often made of wood, usually with drawers, shelves, and doors, once served as clothes closets in homes without built-in closets. Today's armoires have hanging poles as well as shelves and drawers. I recommend this highly versatile piece of furniture. Use it for decoration as well as for the central storage unit in any room in the house. I think you'll find it presents numerous possibilities for use.

Use an armoire in a family room or living room to hide a television, house your stereo and video equipment, store games and activity kits, organize your hobby equipment, file your music and instruments, and hold your family archives.

In a bedroom use an armoire for clothing storage, as an accessory garage for all those purses, shoes, scarves, and jewelry, and as a makeup center. It's also an ideal place to house your television and stereo, if you like to have these in the bedroom.

In a bathroom use an armoire to store your linens, supplied with scented papers that will keep everything smelling sunshine fresh. It's also a handy place to keep cleaning supplies. And store all those products for your hair, shaving, and manicure supplies. Keep a robe and slippers there to follow a relaxing bath.

Use an armoire in a guest room. Gain more storage in your guest room by using an armoire to provide hanging space and storage shelves for guests. And tuck in a robe, towels, and extra pillows for your visitors. That way items can be hidden away but become quickly accessible when needed. Include an armoire in a home office to encompass papers, books, in- and out-boxes, and other supplies. Or make the armoire a home office itself, outfitting it to hold your computer, printer, and fax machine. Open it and you have your office. Close it and your room reveals not a trace of your work.

An armoire is especially useful in a child's room for providing shelving and drawers. Hang those tiny clothes from a top pole or keep them folded on shelves. Use baskets to hold little socks and booties. Put toys on a lower shelf within easy reach of your child. Close the door and the room looks neat. As your child grows, you can turn the armoire into a homework center to store books, papers, reference books, pens, and pencils. An armoire is a good furniture piece that can transition with your child as he grows and even go with him to his own apartment.

TOOLS YOU NEED

▶ Remember as a child covering an old cigar box with construction paper to store your pencils and crayons for your desk at school? That idea has been replicated these days by store-bought paper- and fabric-covered boxes. Use them to store photos until you can put them in albums, to hold hats and scarves, as well as sewing supplies. Don't like the ones available in stores? Cover craft-store boxes with wallpaper samples or fabric scraps.

▲ An armoire used for storing decorative pieces

Is your kitchen short on cupboards? I love to use an armoire as a pantry to store cooking and baking supplies that ordinarily would be placed in cabinets. An armoire can also hide pots and pans, kitchen dishes, and glasses. Do you have a dining room table but no china cabinet or sideboard? Try an armoire to store china, crystal, silver, seasonal tableware, and decorative pieces. Lay tablecloths, napkins, and table runners flat on armoire shelves so they don't get creased. Seasonal and special-occasion items can go on less reachable shelves, saving more accessible armoire shelves for the things you use every day.

If you have space in your hallway, entry, or mudroom, an armoire is handy for setting up a gift-wrap headquarters. Keep wrapping paper, tissue paper, bows, tags, and other package decorations in baskets or boxes, and use the armoire to hide presents you buy ahead of time. (Just keep the doors shut so prying eyes can't spy them.)

Umbrellas, hats, scarves, gloves, and mittens, as well as backpacks, sports equipment, and other paraphernalia your family requires can be tucked out of sight in an armoire. Give each family member a shelf or a part of a shelf with a name sticker, making it easier to find items on the way out the door in the morning or to after-school activities.

Store It Someplace Else

It's time not only to think outside the usual places to store things, but outside customary living spaces as well. This leaves the garage, attic, basement, utility room, and outside storage building. There are things that just don't need to be stored inside the main house—even if you have the room.

First, clear out those additional spaces. It may be that you've been keeping things you just don't need anymore. Some of the nicest innovations I've seen in years, the prelit artificial Christmas tree and other seasonal decorations with built-in bulbs, have made a lot of what we previously used for holiday decorating passé. Soon after the first prelit tree came on the market, I started noticing older artificial trees showing up in secondhand and thrift stores and put out on garbage-pickup day. Who needs all the hassle of untangling strings of lights, figuring out which bulb doesn't work, then having to string the tree properly? Now you no longer need those boxes of lights and all the accompanying paraphernalia. Donate these to a charity or put them out with the trash and buy a new prelit tree.

Clear your garage, utility room, and outside storage building of half-empty paint cans and cleaning and decorating materials. They're probably not only unusable now, but they may even pose a fire hazard. If you have old fertilizers and other gardening supplies, some of these may have passed their effectiveness date and even become dangerous. Recycle or discard all such materials in a proper manner (check with your local fire department).

Use the attic for long-term storing only. Unless you really enjoy climbing up the steps to your attic, try to put only items there that you retrieve once or twice a year. Whatever you do put in the attic should be stored in sturdy, closed boxes, even sealed to protect against insects, moisture, or dust. Most people put seasonal decorating items in the attic along with larger items used once or twice a year, such as skis for a family vacation or a trunk of memorabilia that just can't be parted with. A recent innovation that facilitates lifting heavy items into the attic safely consists of a special mechanical lift that can be retrofitted to your attic door.

Decide on the best solution for storing your family's sports equipment. Establish a special area of your garage for any sports equipment your family uses often, such as bicycles, tricycles,

ELSEWHERE ON THE WEB

▶ For the ultimate in closet organization, call in the experts. Be ready to part with a lot of money but end up with a closet you'll want to live in. The National Closet Group (www.closets.com), Configurations by Rubbermaid (www.rubbermaidcloset.com), and California Closets (www.calclosets.com) are just some of the companies that want to get your life in order, starting with the closets. Most such companies sell their products for do-it-yourselfers or can professionally install their components.

scooters, and skateboards. Remember the possibility of vertical storage, too: Hang up adult bikes on a wall (if you can) in order to free up space on the floor. Use metal baskets to hold basketballs, baseballs, gloves, and hockey sticks. This will not only free up space in your home but promote safety. We've all heard too many stories of kids getting hurt playing with sports equipment in the house.

A utility room is worthwhile and doesn't have to be ugly. Put shelves over your washing machine and dryer to hold containers of laundry detergent, fabric softener, and bleach. Remove these from the top of appliances so you have a place to fold your laundry there. Shelves in the utility room can also store items that you don't want to have to retrieve from the attic, such as holiday decorations, party punch bowls, and the turkey deep fryer. Other possibilities will suggest themselves as long as you don't categorize the space as only for laundry items.

Let's face it: The garage is where extra stuff seems to end up. I think it's interesting that people store all their junk in the garage while leaving such a valuable asset as their car outside. Before you know it, the car can no longer fit in the garage. Maybe that's why people starting adding onto garages even before they had second cars in the family.

Safety is an important issue in the garage. Too often people are tired when they arrive home and shouldn't have to worry about tripping over something or knocking something over on their way from the car into the house. In some areas insects, even snakes, have gotten into the garage and then into the house because people leave their garage doors open during the day. So keeping the garage as clear of clutter as possible is a sensible idea.

Increasingly companies are getting into the business of helping people organize and store things in the garage. Check out the

WHAT'S HOT

▶ Don't spend your valuable time looking for things. With a label maker you can punch out beautifully printed labels for everything you have stored. Attach labels identifying storage boxes in the garage, shoe boxes in hall closets, boxes with photos and slides, shelves that organize bed linen sizes, and towels hanging in the bath. Wherever you put a printed label, items will stay organized.

▶ **NO ONE IS SEPARATE** from all the activities in this clean open space. The wall of windows lights the space all day.

◀ TRADITIONAL PIECES warm up this family dining room. Add a collection of baskets and a rooster for a French Country flair.

▶ NOTICE HOW the light cabinetry, white counters, and open space provide amazing workspace in this kitchen.

◀ SMOOTH
CURVING LINES
and dark granite
counters set this
contemporary
kitchen apart.

▶THIS ROOM
IS DECORATED
for tea parties,
playing with dolls,
sleepovers, and all
the fun things little
girls like to do.

► WOULDN'T YOU LOVE to have a comfortable seating area in your bedroom? If you have the space, even a comfy chair works well. See how comforting and warm the soft yellow is.

▼ RED AND WHITE floral toile fabric on all the soft goods provide the color in this charming bedroom.

◀ DELICATE ENGLISH FLORAL
prints combine on this classic four-
poster bed. The soft cream walls
provide a delicate background.

▲ BLUE AND DOVE GREY
come together in this sophisticated
bedroom. The upholstered headboard
is great for resting against to read.

▲ SMALL OCTAGONAL FLOOR TILES, a soaking tub, and pedestal sink are elements of a classic bath. The chocolate swag at the window instantly makes it formal and elegant.

▶ THIS PRIVATE SANCTUARY has marble floor tile and tub surround, and a clear glass shower enclosure.

variety of large covered plastic storage bins, some even featuring wheels for ease of movement, which can be kept in the garage. Always keep in mind the use of vertical space by mounting shelves along the walls in the garage. Look into recycling old kitchen cabinets from a home recycling center or buy inexpensive unfinished ones from a home improvement store. They're invaluable for hiding items you don't want to display on open shelving. Premade metal shelving that hangs from the ceiling can be installed to gain more storage space. Use this solution for items you don't need to access every day, since you'll need a stepladder to reach them.

Things are really out of sight under the bed. Think about it: That space under the bed is just wasted space. Why can't it be used for storage, especially in a space-challenged home or apartment? Use a tape measure to measure how much space you have under the bed. Then look in a home improvement store for flat plastic bins designed for just this use. Some even come with wheels so they are easy to pull out and push back under the bed.

I helped a client create clever under-the-bed storage in her child's room by reusing drawers from an old chest of drawers. We painted these bright primary colors to match the room, then attached small rolling wheels we found at a hardware store to the bottom. Now her son pulls out the drawers by their handles to get his toys. When it's time to clean his room, he just pushes the drawers back under the bed.

I once helped another client pare down the number of books in her bookshelves. The remainder she couldn't part with was put in a rolling plastic container under her bed. She reports that one night when she couldn't sleep, she found it easy to reach under the bed for a favorite book to reread without having to get out of bed.

ELSEWHERE ON THE WEB

▶ Companies are jumping on the organization bandwagon, even for the garage. Whirlpool takes garage organization to a new level with its Gladiator GarageWorks. Storage cabinets come with rugged, industrial-looking fronts for a garage. Maple-topped cabinets provide storage. Drinks and other items can be stored in a refrigerator with tread-plated construction. See the system at www.gladiatorgw .com.

Other storage places that are out of sight are under the stairs or in a dry basement. I've seen people hang a curtain from the ceiling to conceal a storage area behind a bed. Just use your imagination if you're determined to keep items but storage space is limited.

Keeping It Organized

Once you've restored order to your home, you resolve not to let it get cluttered again. Now that you know how things became disorganized and cluttered to begin with, you don't want to backslide. If you have children, it's particularly important to show them how to live without clutter. Once you live for a while in a more serene environment with fewer things around, you'll want to take steps to keep it that way.

If you can get everyone who lives in the house to join you in keeping your home clutter free and organized, you can achieve that goal. If you've planned for a place for everything, the first thing to do is to make it a family rule that things are put back in their places right away. I helped one family decorate a charming mudroom for their children in which we included hooks on one wall for backpacks and jackets. The family rule was that the backpacks could not be found on the floor or in any other part of the house, else the child it belonged to had to do an extra chore. Mom reported that it took only one infraction of the rule for the kids to learn not to do it again.

Decluttering is not a one-time event. Now that you've gotten rid of clothes and other belongings you weren't using, don't stop. Just as people who have taken off weight need to remain vigilant, be careful not to bring in more things to fill your space. Some people find it helpful to abide by the rule that every time they buy a new item—whether a book, an item of clothing, or a piece of

▶ Set aside half a day occasionally to go through your closets. Move the things you use regularly to one side of the rack. Check that everything is clean. If not, get it cleaned. Taking one item at a time, decide what to do about it. Does it fit? Does it go with something? Do you still like it? Is it still in style? If the answers are yes, put it with the keepers. If the answer is no, out it goes.

furniture—one of the same kind has to go out the door. We're always hearing that people wear 20 percent of their clothes 80 percent of the time. Circulate the clothing in your closet so you wear more of it. After all, isn't that why you bought it? Try a handy little tip I once picked up at a women's business conference: Lay out your wardrobe on your bed and look for interesting combinations you might not have thought of. Then wear those combinations and get rid of items that no longer work. You'll be surprised at what you can give up—and how much more wisely you'll shop next time.

Keep an eye on what your children have outgrown and then donate it as soon as possible. I try to do a seasonal sweep of my closet and donate warm jackets in time for secondhand shops to have them on hand for cold weather. When you buy a new jacket for your child, keep last year's for playing in the yard or for more casual occasions. Then next time around donate that second jacket, putting last year's in second place. You'll both be saving on closet space and making a donation to a secondhand store for some other child.

Keep paper contained. Paper can quickly accumulate. It seems to multiply the moment you look away. Put junk mail immediately in the recycling bin, and set aside your bills in a spot for paying. Have a place to organize receipts, whether manually or electronically. I have a friend who uses back-of-the-door shoe organizers with pockets to hold her bills and receipts. She likes the fact that it's inexpensive and also tucked out of sight except when she goes behind the door to use it. I recommend investing as much time and money as you can afford in working out a system of containing paper. You won't regret it, I promise.

If you work at home, you may find that personal paperwork and bills get mixed with your office paperwork. Establish a place and method to store personal and work items separately to save

WHAT'S HOT

▶ Plan a party with friends who will help you clear things out. I have a number of friends who are empty nesters, thinking about downsizing into smaller, more manageable homes. But the thought of packing everything is just too much, so they stay in their too-big homes. Your friends will understand and be helpful since they're probably in the same situation. Offer to reciprocate when you're done. Anything that gets dumped is up for grabs.

confusion. Keep pens, your checkbook, and stamps always in the same place so you can pay bills quickly and easily (if not electronically). Tax receipts and records don't have to be kept for twenty years. Find out how long your tax preparer would like you to keep these on hand and then each year when you file a new return, shred and recycle the oldest one.

Rework your closet space. Every person has different needs for her closet. You might need more room for shoes than someone else, so having lots of shoe caddies would be a priority for you. Some people, especially if they don't have a big bedroom, like to use shelves to store their folded sweaters, T-shirts, and jeans instead of hanging them up or putting them in a chest of drawers. Think about building extra shelves inside your closet, extending all the way to the ceiling if necessary. Mount a second pole so you can hang shirts and jackets on top and skirts and pants below, for maximum storage. Look into the many closet organization systems you can buy, install one yourself, or hire a closet organization company to do it for you. This will be money well-spent.

Get Linked

Because getting rid of clutter is so essential for having a beautiful home, I've written about it extensively on my Web site. You'll find more helpful information at the following links.

RECRUIT YOUR KIDS TO HELP ORGANIZE THEIR ROOM

Get your kids involved in cleaning things up, and they'll be more enthusiastic about keeping it that way.
http://about.com/interiordec/kidsorganize

STORAGE SOLUTIONS FOR HOLIDAY DECORATIONS

Get good tips on putting holiday decorations away for next year.
http://about.com/interiordec/holidaystorage

Chapter 13

Window and Wall Treatments

Drapes and Curtains

Many people don't know what to do about window treatments. They're not sure if they should match the walls, contrast them, or pick up on a color in the furniture upholstery. And what kind of curtains? If there's a budget for custom draperies, you'll do a lot of looking through samples and styles, but at least a professional's in charge.

Privacy is essential. Unless you live miles away from other people, you need a way to keep your windows covered much of the time. Window coverings also serve to keep too much sun from fading furniture and carpets. They also keep summer heat out and home heating in when the weather is cold outside.

I like to help homeowners explore the numerous options so they won't just choose habitual solutions for their windows. Curtains and drapes, made of fabric hung from a rod at the top of a window, are the most popular window treatment. Drawn open,

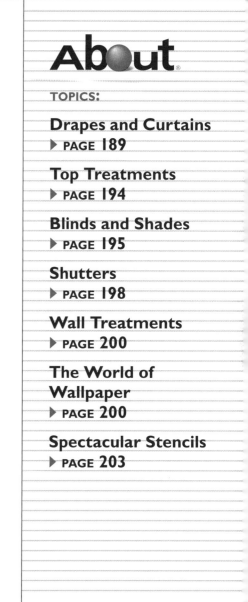

they let in the view; closed, they make your room cozy and private. Linings help prevent fading. Thermal linings retain heat in rooms during the winter while keeping out heat in summer. Blackout linings block all light so you can sleep in a darkened room at all hours of the day. Their extra expense is worth it. It doesn't matter how heavy your curtain material is—only linings will protect your furnishings from sun damage.

▶ These days many people take steps to protect themselves, their furniture, and their homes from harmful ultraviolet (UV) rays of the sun. The life span of personal possessions is doubled by using protective film to cover windows. Although destructive rays are blocked, daylight gets through, privacy is insured, cooling costs are reduced, and safety is enhanced as treated glass becomes more shatter-resistant. I recommend you have this window treatment professionally done to avoid wrinkles in the application.

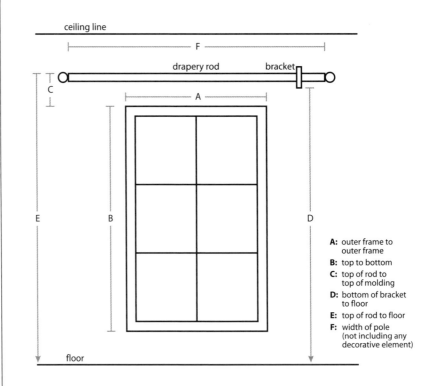

A: outer frame to outer frame
B: top to bottom
C: top of rod to top of molding
D: bottom of bracket to floor
E: top of rod to floor
F: width of pole (not including any decorative element)

▲ Measure before hanging rod and window treatments

Decide how formal or informal you want your curtains to be and then measure your windows. Hanging curtains near the ceiling is a trick for making a room look higher. Most people opt for hanging curtains a few inches above the top of a window and extending the rod several inches from each side. Next consider whether you want your curtains to end at the bottom of a window or hang floor-length. Be sure to measure width and length before you shop and take written measurements with you. It's hard to rely on memory when you're confronted by all the choices in a fabric store.

Window treatments finish off a room. They add color, texture, and style as well as privacy. They are also the first place to start if you're not ready to replace furniture. New curtains can dramatically change the look of a room at a lower cost than buying a new sofa, carpeting, or flooring.

Nothing dates a room like dingy drapes or curtains stuck in the 1970s, left hanging because their owners seem to see past them. With myriad choices available in ready- and custom-made draperies, there's no reason to put up with an outmoded style. If you sew, don't forget the bountiful resources of fabric stores, home centers, and **drapery** workrooms.

Making simple drapery panels is not terribly difficult, but it does require careful measuring. To make the job easier, especially if you'll be installing a valance over the panels, finish the panel to the proper length. Then sew drapery pleating tape to the underside of the top of the panels. By gently pulling the strings woven into the tape, you can obtain perfect pencil pleats, smocking pleats, box pleats, and classic pinch pleats. See examples of tapes at www.draperysewing supplies.com/Pleat_Tape_s/12.htm.

TOOLS YOU NEED

▶ If you purchase ready-made curtains, you need to carefully position the curtain rod so the panels hang straight and evenly when they're installed. Measure the length of the panel, the length of your window from top to bottom and side to side, and figure out just where the rod should be hung to show off the curtains (and any window molding) to best advantage and to give you the coverage and privacy you need.

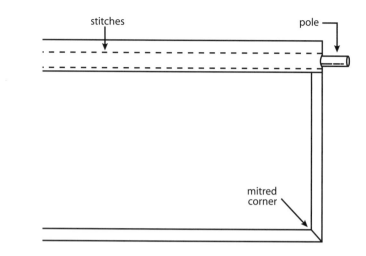

▲ Making your own curtains is simple

▶ When you're ready to install your curtains or draperies, gather your tools so the job proceeds smoothly. You'll need a tape measure, level, drill, screwdriver, anchors, and hammer. Measure carefully to get the markings level, drill holes for brackets, tap an anchor into the holes with a hammer, and screw the brackets into the wall. Set the pole in the brackets and attach the drapery panels or curtains. Spread the full fabric evenly.

You might have questions about what sort of curtains to buy. When it comes to ready-made window treatments, many people opt for simple tabbed **panels** that don't really reflect their taste, just to easily hang some sort of covering on windows. But there are many alternatives to tabbed panels that can markedly enhance your windows. Choose informal fabrics in cotton, linen, and man-made materials. Formal fabrics consist of satin, velvet, and other luxurious materials.

Check the fabrication of the curtains. Are they machine washable or will they need to be dry-cleaned? This is an important consideration since dry-cleaning requires additional time and expense. Are the curtains lined? If your windows get direct sunlight, you'll need lining. Finally, make sure your store will allow you to return purchased curtains if you discover they just don't look right at home.

If you don't have existing curtain hardware, you'll need to install it. Follow directions for the particular kind of hardware you buy. Most require a drill and screw anchors to keep the hardware from pulling out of a plaster wall. Using a level will ensure that your curtains hang straight rather than crooked.

Decorative window hardware is made to be seen. Other types of hardware are better covered. Which kind you'll use depends on the formality of your room and the window treatment you choose. Hardware is steadily becoming more attractive so that it stands out on the wall. Finials on the ends of curtain rods can be made of beautifully carved wood, metal, or glass. I've seen blown Murano glass finials used that were lovelier than the hanging curtains.

To support heavy draperies, be sure to buy sturdy hardware. However, be careful not to mix overpowering hardware with lightweight curtains or use it in too small a room. Look for hardware that has an inside rod for hanging sheers behind draperies, if this is the look you want.

Café curtains can be a good choice for an informal decorating style. When you want a curtain at the window to set it off but don't need complete privacy, consider a café curtain. These have a valance—in the form of a ruffled strip of curtain at the top of the window—and a bottom curtain that covers the lower half of the window. They fit well in kitchens, breakfast nooks, and informal dining areas.

It's important to think about safety when you're planning your window treatments. For a child's room, consider shades or short curtains instead of long curtains that can be pulled down. Since dangling cords pose a safety hazard for small children, find blinds that come with safety cords.

In a safety innovation, many blinds and shades now come with remote controls instead of cords. The remote control device adds to the cost, but the safety aspect can be worth it. The fact that you

ELSEWHERE ON THE WEB

▶ You can make your own curtains and drapes, buy them ready-made, or have them custom-made for your home. In any case, you'll need to measure the window, surrounding walls, window frame, and height of ceiling to get the perfect fit. For information on measuring your window, visit http://todoes.com/DP-measure.html. If you decide to have draperies custom-made, the folks from the workroom will want to come to your home to measure before giving an estimate.

I can never seem to get my curtains to hang well with tiebacks. Are there any rules about where to place tiebacks?

▶ Definitely. Tiebacks should be placed either one-third of the way down from the top of the drapery panel or one-third of the way up from the bottom hem. If you follow this rule, both the top and bottom portions of the curtain will have a soft, smooth curve, and the panel will fall gracefully.

don't have to get up to close shades as you sit rocking your baby is a useful feature as well.

Top Treatments

Even the most ordinary pair of ready-made curtains can be dressed up with window top treatments. These include valances, swags, **cornice** boxes, ruffling, shirring, and adding special embellishments like fringe or trim. Window adornment works well in a traditional or formal room where you want additional detail and interest.

Swags are considered an easy window top treatment. All you have to do is drape material over the top of your curtain rod, right? Well, not exactly. It's a bit harder than it looks to drape the fabric so that it looks graceful and even. And you want to use pretty fabric, not just anything. But swags mean no sewing (unless rough edges show on the draped fabric), and they're easy enough to take down and replace. I like swags for adding a seasonal touch to a room. If you have neutral or fairly plain draperies or curtains, try a swag of flowery chiffon for spring, fabric printed with colorful flowers or paisley for summer, linen twined with a garland of silk leaves for autumn, and—of course—glistening satin swags tied on each side with silk poinsettias or a cluster of shiny Christmas ornaments for winter.

Valances cover the top of a window and the drapery hardware. A valance can be made of the same or of contrasting material as the draperies. A casing is often sewn at the top of the valance so the fabric can be gathered on a curtain rod. Add trim for your valance for a dramatic statement.

Cornice boxes make a special window treatment. These usually have to be custom-built to fit windows since they're not something you can find ready-made at a store. But the simple box-style construction is a project the average do-it-yourselfer can manage. Just think of building a rectangular box but leaving off the two long sides of the rectangle, then installing at the top of your window using L-brackets. These were very popular years ago and are currently undergoing a resurgence of interest as a way to add a custom look to a room. You can either paint them or cover them with bunting and then fabric, stapling to secure it in place. The fabric can be the same as your bedspread or even the curtains. You can cut a decorative edge along the bottom front and sides and paint or stencil the wood. Sit back and wait for compliments.

Blinds and Shades

Blinds are referred to as "hard" window treatments. A series of slats of wood or plastic (or other man-made materials), blinds can be louvered open or shut. Vertical and horizontal blinds give you privacy and light control with a clean, sleek look. Many people like them because they're not fussy and are very easy to clean: Just swipe them with a damp cloth or use one of the clever new antistatic innovations that have made feather dusters a thing of the past. Gone, too, is the old-fashioned look of the Venetian blinds you may remember from your grandmother's house. Today's blinds come in materials such as wood, vinyl, aluminum, and bamboo. They can roll up, open like curtains (vertical blinds, discussed in an upcoming section), and even come with their own valances.

I've seen blinds in a wide range of colors installed in very different types of rooms. Use hard window treatments in a room where drapes and curtains would just be too fussy. For instance, put bamboo blinds in a contemporary or ethnic inspired room. Use them for rooms with a casual feeling, like a family room. They're also appropriate for entries, garages, offices, and workshops. Whatever

▶ It's important for a window valance to be in proper proportion to the window treatment. Measure from the top of the drapery to the floor or, for shorter curtains, to the window sill. Divide the measurement by five or six to obtain the proper length for a valance. If the window is wide, deeper is better. Test the length by taping newspaper where the valance will be installed. Adjust as needed.

type of blind you choose, you'll have a durable, fashionable treatment for your window that fits into most decorating budgets, from ready-made blinds for the thrifty shopper to custom-made ones for a more extravagant budget.

Miniblinds can be used by themselves or under curtains. Bamboo or matchstick blinds are a natural window covering for a casual room or one with an ethnic flair. Wooden blinds are perfect for a family room or any room where you want some decorating punch.

Although it's always important to measure carefully, this is particularly crucial when you're buying blinds for your windows. Be off by a ½" on curtains and it's not a big problem. Do it with blinds and it's a disaster: Blinds are actually measured to the nearest eighth of an inch. The most important thing is to decide whether you're doing an inside or an outside mount. Inside mount entails installing the blinds within the window frame opening; outside mount involves installing the blinds outside the window opening or on the front of the window frame.

Blinds usually look best installed inside the window but are sometimes installed outside the window opening to hide any imperfections the window or frame has. Be careful not to extend blinds too much past the window opening, since when light shines through it will look odd to see wall behind the blind. Although inside mounts are used with most blinds, outside mounts are usually done for blinds on a sliding glass door, a French door, or on certain style windows like Anderson windows.

Consider the details of the blinds you choose. Aluminum miniblinds have been popular for some time because they come in a variety of colors and are a lightweight and inexpensive window treatment. When you want to let the view in, you can raise them; when you want privacy, you can lower them. An added advantage is that when you want to let in just a little light but don't want to

ELSEWHERE ON THE WEB

▶ An upholstered cornice box at the top of your window treatment gives a professional and finished look. This is a project for a confident do-it-yourselfer. Choose the perfect fabric for your room, buy the supplies, and follow the step-by-step instructions offered by the Fabric Workshop at www .fabricworkshop.com/cornice1 .htm. You can build a straight box cornice or add a scrolled bottom edge, trim it with cording or fringe, and have a custom look.

lose your privacy, you can simply use the control cord to tilt the slats to the degree of light you want to enter.

Choose all-natural blinds for an especially informal look. Bamboo blinds offer a striking combination of simplicity and function that I find appealing. Beware, however, that bamboo blinds do not provide complete privacy. Bamboo grows more quickly than hardwood trees and has been embraced as a renewable resource by designers and homeowners who support the green building movement.

Vertical blinds offer a sleek window treatment. They provide ideal light control and privacy, opening and closing like draperies. The new generation of vertical blinds have an updated contemporary look. They also create a nice optical illusion by making a room look bigger and a ceiling seem higher.

Use vertical blinds on sliding glass doors instead of fussy drapes, and you'll find yourself focusing on the view more. They come in a wide range of styles and are easy to clean. I don't like the fact that they make noise when opening and closing as well as when windows are open, since the vertical slats sometimes sway in breezes. It's worth keeping in mind the pros and cons of vertical blinds.

Take a look at fabric specialty shades, which I like to use to freshen up a room. Balloon shades with their puffy elegance add a romantic touch to a room. Although balloon shades can block light and provide privacy when lowered, they are often used to cover just the top part of a window. Honeycomb shades are custom-pleated, two- or three-layer shades that come in sheer or **opaque** materials, some of blackout density. Lower the top and cover the bottom of your windows if you want to let in sunlight without giving up privacy. Elegant Roman shades are made of a

ASK YOUR GUIDE

I want a clean, neat look on my windows but can't afford custom plantation shutters. What are some other options?

▶ The best way to get a similar look is through custom-made wide wooden blinds with slats about 2" wide. You can get a much less expensive, cut-to-size, ready-made imitation with solid vinyl blinds available at home improvement stores. The key to good-looking blinds is accurate measuring and installation. They are fairly easy to install; if you can use a screwdriver, you can put in blinds.

▶ I can't say it enough: Getting the proper measurement for your window blinds is essential. If you measure the width too short, the header for the blind will not span the window and you'll see light on the sides of the blind. Every measurement has to be exact to $\frac{1}{8}$". There's a beneficial tutorial on the Decorating Depot site. They give instructions at www. decoratingdepot.com/ ?f=measure for installation of almost any window covering.

wide range of materials. They needn't only be custom-made these days, either: Fabric stores sell the necessary cablelike pull strings and directions to make Roman shades at home in very little time.

Install balloon shades on the outside of the window. They hang from a board held at the top of a window using L-brackets. Determine the actual width you desire and cut a board that size. Cover it with drapery-lining fabric or other fabric. Attach O-rings to the underside of the board, spacing them to correspond with the cords on the fabric panel. Attach the board to the wall using L-brackets extending equidistantly from each side of the window frame. Then attach the finished strung shade to the mounting board with Velcro or staples. Thread the shade cording through the O-rings on the panel and through to the side on which you'll draw the blind.

Roman shades are hung the same way, although occasionally they are hung inside. For inside mounts, most have a bracket that is screwed into the wall, and then each side of the shade slides down into an opening in the bracket. The installation is fairly easy, requiring no drill, screw anchors, or level. Check the directions on the package. Honeycomb shades are almost always hung inside, although they can be hung outside the same way as Roman shades.

Roller shades made of plastic or other man-made materials were rather industrial when they first came out years ago, but now they're more fashionable and functional. These shades are attached to a roller and can be pulled down from the top of a window. Use these shades under nonlined curtains to protect furnishings. Install roller shades the same way as other inside shades. If your window is not a standard size, plastic or other man-made shades can be cut to order at some stores.

Shutters

I don't think there's anything that makes a more charming window treatment than wooden shutters. They add an architectural element to your room that is not only beautiful but helps save energy by controlling light and heat. Wooden shutters also help with sound insulation. And since people love them so much, they add to the value of your home when you sell it.

Shutters come in a variety of **louver** sizes from 1⅞" to 3½". Narrow slats are best for small windows and small rooms. The wide plantation shutters make a bold statement on larger windows and in large rooms. They also come in a wide range of stains from light to dark and can also be painted. Most people prefer white in painted shutters because these brighten a room so much, but you can also go with a neutral color. Visit a home improvement store to check out the various wooden shutter styles. Café style means the shutters are mounted on the lower half of a window. For privacy, put a curtain or valance at the top. White shutters look charming in cottage-style rooms. I also like them in a baby's room because of their simplicity and neat lines. And breakfast nooks and kitchens are perfect places for café-style wooden shutters.

If you have decided to invest in shutters, don't try to cut corners. Visit a shutter store, select your favorite style, then have a professional come to your home to measure and make plans for installation. Unless you're very experienced, installing large shutters (especially plantation shutters) is a job for a professional.

Full window shutters give a room privacy. If you have a room with a bad view, you have a too-close neighbor, or you live in a very cold or hot climate, consider installing a full window shutter. This style works well in a den or office, no matter what style decorating is used.

If you don't like the hard look of full wood shutters but also don't want the exposure of a café-style wooden shutter, try using a woven insert. I've seen a homeowner remove the remaining louvers from broken shutters she found at a yard sale, then glue in fabric inserts to match her family room.

TOOLS YOU NEED

▶ Vacuum blinds with a dust head attachment or use a soft dusting cloth, tilting regular blinds up and down (or right to left with verticals). The new chemically treated dust cloths work well on blinds (if they're not made of cloth or certain man-made materials). If your blinds are very dirty, you can detach the blades and clean them in your bathtub filled with soapy water. Rinse completely and dry before rehanging.

▶ The invention of the printing press and of machine-made paper brought wallpaper to ordinary people's homes. After almost a decade of being out of favor, wallpaper is returning in a big way to home decorating. Believe it or not, even texturized wallpaper is returning, providing a soft, touchable feel to walls. You can read more about the history of the development and design of wallpaper at www.wallpaperinstaller.com/wallpaper_history.html. It's true that everything old is new again.

Wall Treatments

There are so many ways to get a new look in your home through furniture, flooring, window treatments, and lighting that walls are sometimes neglected. However, when you decorate walls, you can change the look of a room dramatically with very little money, time, and effort. Perhaps it's this significant change that many people fear when decorating. But if you start small and proceed carefully, you'll be fine. Even if you decide what you're doing isn't what you visualized, you can probably fix it. (On the other hand, don't be too hasty to tear down a wall, since it takes money and effort to put another one up!)

Go back to that decorating file you started in Chapter 4. Have you added photos of rooms that show different wall treatments? I've clipped photos of walls through the years that I love to use for inspiration. These involve paint treatments, wallpaper, and stencils.

The World of Wallpaper

There's a world of styles in wallpaper sample books in your local home improvement store, offering countless possibilities for changing the look of a room. These sample books include photos of actual rooms that designers have created.

If you have wall surfaces with problems, such as dated paneling or less-than-smooth plaster, wallpaper offers a quick, easy, inexpensive solution that paint won't cover. There is even a wallpaper liner to make a smooth surface for better application of wallpaper and for camouflaging imperfections.

Some people shy away from wallpaper because they've seen others struggle to take old wallpaper off. But that's because those people were dealing with wallpaper that was years old, sometimes decades so. Today's wallpapers are so much easier to put up and easier to take down that they bear looking into.

(Instructions on how to install wallpaper are included later in this chapter.)

Bring your decorating file with you when you look at wallpaper samples. That way you can compare a paint chip or fabric sample to a wallpaper sample. Be sure to note which samples you like and the manufacturer, title of the book, and page number where you found them. (There are so many books, it's easy to lose track of your source.)

Look for room decorating ideas as you scan the books, which are rich in photos of the latest wallpaper applications, even more than in decorating magazines or on TV shows. Wallpaper companies pay designers hefty fees to incorporate wallpaper products in actual settings. Love a nautical look for a bedroom? Try a wallpaper mural of portholes with ocean views. This is an artful way of introducing a view in a room without one while matching your décor.

Wallpaper is ideal for a cottage-style room. A cozy cottage room requires texture, color, and interest, which wallpaper provides beautifully. Try mixing florals and prints or stripes. If you're hesitant to apply a faux painting treatment to your walls, there are new wall coverings designed to look like faux painted finishes. Leather and suede, metallic, strié, sponging, and Venetian plaster are painting techniques you can now get in wallpaper. How about delicate clouds on the ceiling? The sky's the limit.

Not ready for an entire room of wallpaper? No problem. I like to use wallpaper on a focal wall for a dramatic touch. You can later extend it to the rest of the room. Use decorative molding to frame panels of wallpaper in a dining or living room for an elegant look. Add sconces to light up the framed areas.

WHAT'S HOT

▶ Natural organic wallpapers made of grass cloth, linen, leather, suede, and cork are hot new wallpaper trends—again. Reflective metallics are back in more subtle contemporary designs and work well in dark rooms. Many types of wallpaper are pretreated for easy dusting and spot removal, making them practical for a kitchen. Acoustical wallpapers help to cut down on the amount of noise in a room.

It's a good idea to start small, with a wallpaper border. Discovering how easy a wallpaper border is to hang (and how good it looks) can inspire you to take on a full wallpaper project. A child's room is a smart place for a border, enabling you to change the theme as your child grows. Put the border along the ceiling or slightly below. To create the look of a chair railing around the room, hang the border about one-third of the way up from the floor.

For tips on measuring and estimating how much wallpaper to buy, the guide at www.wallcoverings.org/residential/estimating.html is helpful.

Wallpaper installation is easy if you first spend a little time preparing the walls. If the walls are painted, it's important to wash them first; experts recommend a solution of trisodium phosphate, available at the hardware store. Rinse with water and let dry. If the walls are new drywall, first prime them with drywall primer or sizer. Are the walls already wallpapered? You can wallpaper over them but be sure to wipe off dried old paste and let it dry, then sand any imperfections.

Once you've measured the walls carefully, cut the wallpaper panels to size, allowing 2" extra at the top and bottom. Be sure to match any pattern on the panels before you cut the paper.

Most wallpapers on the market come pre-pasted. To activate the paste, slide the loosely rolled panel of wallpaper into a plastic tray of water or in a bathtub filled with lukewarm water. After the wallpaper is wet and the paste activated, gently fold the wet, pasted sides together, taking care not to crease the paper. This is called "booking" the wallpaper and makes it easier to carry to the wall. Prepare only one roll at a time as you work so the paste doesn't dry out before you apply the wallpaper. Use a level to determine a straight vertical line, marking the wall with a pencil. Then gently unfold the wallpaper against the wall, starting from the top of the wall and working down, smoothing out any air bubbles that appear. Be sure to match up wallpaper if you have a repeating pattern. Using a straight blade razor, carefully cut off the excess paper at the ceiling and baseboard. These instructions are very basic. For more detailed tips on wallpaper installing techniques, see www.ehow.com/how_1662_hang-wallpaper.html.

Spectacular Stencils

Paint and wallpaper are not the only wall treatments for your rooms. Stencils combine a painted surface with images or words in designs sometimes inspired by wallpaper. Applying stencils is one of the most enjoyable home decorating techniques I've used, a way to play artist even if you think you're not creative or are all thumbs. You can stencil all sorts of designs, such as flowers and leaves, border designs, and words.

Stencils, which were popular in colonial times, until recently consistently of simple objects like ducks and fruit, usually seen only in homes with a country decorating style. But no more. Stencils have undergone a transformation. Stencils are an appealing alternative if you don't want to make a commitment to wallpaper or to a paint treatment. Abundant choices in stencils are available from home improvement stores, craft stores, and the Internet. If you're a little creative, you can duplicate a design by cutting your own stencil out of plain Mylar sheets. Simply place the Mylar over the design you like and cut out with an X-acto knife. I've used stencils in every room of the house: a beautiful repeating stencil of a leaf in dreamy greens for a bedroom; stylistic seahorses in a bathroom; words to inspire for a writer's office, and baseballs and bats in a boy's bedroom.

Stenciled designs are turning up everywhere. Stencil leaves or flowers on your bedroom wall and repeat the designs on curtains, linens, or a lampshade for a coordinated look. An old dresser or armoire looks new with designs stenciled on drawers. Stencil words on walls, such as adding a phrase like "Sweet Dreams" over a baby's crib, stenciling the alphabet in a child's room, or including a pet's name on a dog bed. The options are as varied as your imagination.

Get Linked

There is a wide range of ways to use window treatments and wall finishes to create a unique room. You'll find more articles and pictures on my Interior Decorating site on About.com.

ALL ABOUT WINDOW COVERINGS

Here is my site's index to window coverings, including links to product manufacturers and information on installation, products, and design resources.

↗ http://about.com/interiordec/windowcover

EVERYTHING YOU NEED TO KNOW ABOUT BUYING WALLPAPER

Read about measuring, shopping for, choosing, and buying wallpaper.

↗ http://about.com/interiordec/wallpapertips

Chapter 14

Flooring: From Hardwood to Carpeting

The Importance of Flooring

This chapter addresses the subject of flooring, one of the most important components of a room's look but an area often neglected in decorating projects. Think back to when you first entered your current home. What aspects caught your eye? Chances are the flooring was one of the first things you noticed. Because flooring covers all of a home's area, it's impossible to ignore its impact. Realtors will tell you that they often lose sales when clients encounter stained or damaged floors and very old carpeting during a showing. Nothing improves the look and value of a home like good flooring.

Choices for flooring abound: natural wood (including exotic woods like bamboo), wood laminates, tile, concrete, vinyl, carpeting, and area rugs. Within these categories, of course, lie numerous options. Just think how many types of wood flooring alone there are, from popular oak to fairly new bamboo. If you're thinking of

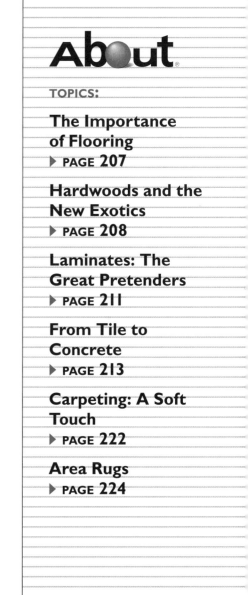

ASK YOUR GUIDE

Do I need to have a professional install a new wood floor, or can I do it myself?

▶ Hardwood flooring is a big investment for any home, so it's important to have a floor installed by someone experienced. Although it is a job you can do yourself, there's a lot you need to learn first. For example, did you know that wood needs to adjust to the temperature and humidity in your home before it's laid? The National Wood Flooring Association (www.woodfloors.org/consumer/findpro.aspx) recommends that you engage a professional to do the work for best results.

replacing flooring, you need to give the matter serious consideration since it can be costly.

Hardwoods and the New Exotics

Many years ago, there were only a few woods used for flooring. People tended to use the type of wood that grew in forests near them. For most American homes, that meant oak or pine, sometimes maple. The strongest wood was selected (if there was a choice), which was then cut into planks for installation. Hundred-year-old wood floors have held up well, as you've seen if you ever visited a historic home. Many grand old homes have beautiful **parquet** and **marquetry** designs that are less frequently reproduced today, due to the time and skill involved.

▲ Hardwood floors: timeless, attractive, and easy to maintain.

Hardwood floors have always been popular, but in recent years they've enjoyed a resurgence in popularity as people return to natural products. Though a traditional choice, wood floors suit all decorating styles since they provide a neutral background. Wood is also popular as a material because it is easy to clean and to maintain. Vacuum or sweep with one of the new dust magnet brooms on a regular basis. Water should never be used to clean a wood floor. Prevent scratches from dirt and grit by keeping quality doormats at your front and back doors and insisting your family use them.

Wood floors are a good investment. Primarily used in living rooms, dining rooms, bedrooms, and sometimes in kitchens, wood floors are often a selling point with potential buyers. They are not problem free, since they can become stained, scratched, even lose their color if they're exposed to too much sunlight coming through windows. Compared to other types of flooring, they are not cheap either, though experts estimate they can last fifty years or more when properly cared for.

Wood floors are installed either unfinished or factory-finished. Custom stains and sealers are used on raw wood floors that are finished on the job site. Factory-finished floors can have many more coats of finish applied by comparison. Some manufacturers add aluminum oxide for additional durability. If you're a homeowner with the necessary skills and equipment, you can install a wood floor in your home yourself, although I find most people have a wood floor professionally installed. Prices for hardwood floors vary too widely to estimate here, depending on their availability, supply, and demand. Check with several reputable flooring companies for their best quotes, and find out how long those quotes will be honored.

ELSEWHERE ON THE WEB

▶ The Janka Hardness Test (www.countyfloors.com/about_janka.html) evaluates the hardness of wood floors. The degree of hardness is important to know, according to Bob Formisano, About.com's expert on Home Repair, for choosing the best wood floor for your needs. For example, Formisano notes that a pine floor can be scratched by a dog with long nails. A wood species with a higher rating, such as hickory, maple, oak, or ash, might be a better choice. For more information, read Formisano's article at http://about.com/homerepair/wood floor.

▶ In recent years a home inspection conducted by a professional home inspector has become a crucial step in buying a home. It's important to know the condition of systems in the house. Be sure to obtain a thorough evaluation of flooring, too. This includes carpet and underlying pad as well as hardwood floors. Confirm that a floor is sound and not eaten by termites or beetles. Flooring that shows signs of weakness could be a real liability.

Have your existing wood floors refinished for a new look. If your wood floors are looking tired or exhibit minor damage, it's probably time to have them professionally refinished. Finding a good wood flooring expert to do the job takes some investigation. Since there are many types of wood floors, a floor refinisher who is unqualified can do real damage. Ask for names of reputable floor refinishers at local flooring stores and check the yellow pages of your phone book. As with hiring any professional, check references before hiring someone, and call the **Better Business Bureau** to make sure no complaints have been filed.

If you're having a wood floor refinished, discuss with your flooring expert whether to have the floor stained a lighter or darker color. This is possible to do with certain wood floors, depending on the type of wood, its age, and condition. I've seen floors refinished with a darker stain than the original color, for a gorgeous look.

Be prepared not to walk on the floors for the duration of the job, which might mean vacating the house. Obviously the room undergoing the work has to be completely emptied of furniture. I had a client who was having his floors refinished while simultaneously waiting for new furniture to arrive. Unfortunately, this was delivered right when the workers were in the middle of the refinishing job. The new furniture had to be wrapped in plastic and stored in the garage until the floor was finished and completely dry.

Bamboo is an attractive new flooring material. Who would have thought that bamboo floors would become so popular? Credit not only a handsome surface but also the public's environmental awareness for making bamboo the new darling of flooring. Bamboo is quick growing—it takes just five to six years to reach maturity, unlike hardwood trees. For this reason and because it is self-regenerating, it's considered very eco-friendly.

Bamboo is very durable. It's as hard as maple and more stable than red oak. Bamboo floors are elegant, with a unique grain, and they can be dramatic when stained dark. Contractors who use this wood have told me they're pleased with its flexibility and adaptability to design possibilities. Be sure to have a bamboo floor professionally installed; laying it is not a project for an amateur. Check out bamboo to determine whether it's the type of flooring for you.

Another exotic floor is cork. Cork might seem an unusual material for flooring for those who have only seen it used for wine bottle stoppers and corkboards. But the word about cork is that it's very versatile. It's lightweight, impermeable to liquids and gases, and like bamboo regenerates quickly, so it's good for the environment.

The best features about cork flooring? It's soft and warm, deadens sound, and insulates. Cork comes in planks and tiles with a protective vinyl finish that makes it easy to clean. Additional benefits are that it's antimicrobial and resistant to mold and mildew. On the downside, although it's been known to last for many years even in commercial settings, it can fade in direct sunlight and yellow with age. Moisture can make its seams swell. This flooring needs to be installed by a professional who has worked extensively with it.

Laminates: The Great Pretenders

Woodlike laminate floors have come a long way. I think they're an excellent way to afford a woodlike floor for less money than hardwood. They are also designed to be easily installed by homeowners, which is a distinct budget advantage over traditional wood floors. And many people like the satisfaction of installing a floor themselves. The flooring looks like hardwood but is as easy to care for as a laminate countertop. It can be installed over nearly any surface—plywood, concrete slab, and old vinyl. Though it's been available only since the mid-1990s, hundreds of millions of square

I love the simplicity of laminate flooring but want the look of tile or marble. Is there any way I can get that look?

▶ The designs now available in laminate flooring vary widely. Although most laminate flooring replicates the look of hardwood flooring, you can find patterns that look like tumbled marble, slate, stone, basalt and sand. Shop online at www.bruce.com or www.armstrong.com to view options, then visit your home improvement or flooring store to see in person.

feet of laminate flooring have sold because of its resistance to scratches, burns, dents, and chipping.

Installation is easy using the "free-floating" method, which means laying the flooring on top of a subfloor. Some brands that fit together without glue can actually be taken up and moved along with the furniture to your next home, if you wish. Laminate flooring comes in planks that snap together, and most rooms can be done in a day. Be sure to follow usual instructions to let the flooring "rest" before installing it to avoid problems snapping it together. I think you'll agree that if you can do the physical job of cutting laminate boards with a saw to fit your measurements and then do the work of locking the pieces together, laminate floors are a do-it-yourself dream.

Both hardwood and laminate flooring come in planks of different widths. Narrow planks give a modest look while wide planks, up to 6" or even 8" wide, are luxurious and rare. For a modest home, stick with a high-quality flooring that enhances your decorating scheme and will give you years of wear. For a custom look, consider the various patterns of laminate flooring, including inlaid designs that some companies offer.

Laminate flooring can look like other materials besides wood. Armstrong and other big flooring manufacturers produce laminate flooring that looks like stone and tile. Because the designs on laminate flooring are basically photographs, some floors I have seen look like water or sand. We may well see even homeowner photos pop up one of these days in laminate flooring patterns! Check the options available at your flooring store. Prices for laminate can vary from a few dollars per square foot for a basic product to $15 and up. For a large job, consider going to a discount flooring warehouse for the best deal.

From Tile to Concrete

Tile has never looked better. Yes, tile is a building and decorating material that people have been using for thousands of years to make their homes more livable and beautiful. But have you looked in a tile store at recent innovations? I can tell you that there are exciting trends in tile these days. Floor tiles are bigger and better, stones like marble have become affordable to people with modest budgets, and there's an explosion of interest in luminous, colorful glass tile.

▲ Tile flooring in a modern kitchen

▶ You don't have to settle for a white tile counter or floor ever again. Designer tiles are available with exotic fairy tale themes and expression of the ocean depths. Tile materials range from wood grains and luminous glass to opulent metallics. Textures and edging options abound. There's no excuse for stylistic ruts anymore.

Tile is used everywhere in modern homes—on floors in every room of the house, on walls, backsplashes, and kitchen counters, in bathroom showers, and on bathroom walls. No longer confined to bathrooms, tile has become a decorating wonder that personalizes a home. Love a tile floor? Start at the front door with a tile mosaic inset in the foyer to welcome visitors. Set tile patterns on the floor at an angle or continue foyer tile right into a bedroom. You're only limited by the difficulty of the project.

Love a swirl of color? Use it in your kitchen tile, where it will inspire you to create meals with passion. Replace the kitchen Formica countertop from forty years ago with colorful new tile on countertops and floor. Create an updated bathroom using neutral tile with a rustic finish on the floor, in the shower, along the sides of a new soaking tub, all up the walls. Expensive looks are available for much less money than you might imagine if you're willing to develop the skills needed to install tile yourself. I've seen tile prices range from a little over $1 per tile to $20 or more for imported specialty tiles.

Natural stone floors have an old-world look that can enrich modern homes. Types of stone flooring include marble, granite, slate, travertine, terra cotta, and sandstone. Since no two pieces of natural stone are exactly alike, you're installing something unique. These natural floors are relatively easy-care, although some need applications of a special sealer to prevent stains or surface damage. Natural stone floors also work well in rooms with a contemporary look. Some people like to use this type of flooring throughout the house, not just in kitchens.

Marble tends to be pricey for a flooring choice. If you have the budget for marble, it makes a dramatic statement. Polished marble has a beautiful patina. It's a material that's best left to professional installation. Want marble but find it too costly? Have it installed in a small space for special effect, such as in a foyer or a small powder room, or use it as decorative accents.

Granite, which has become the hottest material for kitchen countertops, is also being used for flooring. It's no wonder. Granite is hard and durable and, like marble, a unique creation of nature. As with marble, no two pieces of granite are identical. Granite colors can be stunning (like the malachite green and black piece I found for a client) as well as soft and subtle. As with marble, this material must be installed by a professional. Since granite is so pricey, you'll probably reserve it for a small space, such as an insert in a kitchen or living room floor.

Slate, which is more rustic than marble or granite, is a fine-grained rock with traces of metal. People love natural materials these days, and they especially love the natural look of slate on floors. Slate goes well in contemporary homes, especially in living rooms and kitchens.

Beige travertine, made of crystallized minerals and limestone, is a stone used in building and flooring from ancient times. The slabs are often marked by pitted holes and troughs in its surface; these are sometimes filled with resin upon installation. Like granite and marble, its natural variations give each piece its own character. Polished travertine has a depth and beauty that adds drama to a home. Travertine is best installed by a professional.

Terra cotta is a popular floor tile in kitchens. Terra cotta tile was once primarily a product of Mexico but now is imported from Italy and Peru as well. Its warm russet coloring varies widely. An installer should mix tiles from a number of boxes so the color won't be concentrated in places. Terra cotta tiles can be installed by a homeowner experienced in cutting tiles to size (using a tile-cutting machine) and laying them.

Another stone tile, called Saturnia and relatively new on the market, comes from Italy's ancient spa areas. The sand holes,

TOOLS YOU NEED

▶ Tile flooring can feel cold and uninviting in homes in colder climes. To solve that problem, install heating coils under the tile. A number of companies manufacture heating elements for flooring, including Warm TouchFloor Warming System (www .warmtilefloors.com/prod ucts.htm), Radiant Floor Warming (www.radiantfloor warming.com/about.html), and NuHeat (www.nuheat .com). Installation is simple as the elements plug into a standard home electrical system. You'll never have cold toes again!

fossils, and other characteristics formed by nature add to its natural appeal. This tile is good in any room inside the house, though it's often used for special effect around a pool.

What could look more natural than sandstone in flooring, with its mixture of sand, minerals, and rock fragments? Ranging in color from sandy and cream to brown and gray (even red and green, depending on where it's found), sandstone was used on large buildings before the invention of concrete in the nineteenth century. Sandstone is good in rooms with a rustic decorating style (such as a living room) as well as for outdoor rooms and patios.

Stone flooring requires specific care. Although natural stone is a hard material, because it's porous it needs a penetrating sealer to keep it from getting stained and damaged. Care is simple and easy. Just use a soft dust mop to remove dust, dirt, and especially grit that can harm the floor. If it should need further cleaning, consult your flooring installer for a cleaner especially formulated for the type of stone used in your home.

Man-made tile can mimic the best of nature's materials. These tiles are rated as nonvitreous, semivitreous, **vitreous**, and impervious, depending on how well they withstand penetration by water and their resistance to abrasion. Whether you buy porcelain or ceramic tile, you're getting a durable product that can last for years. Usually the surface is smoother than some stone floors (one exception being polished marble). Porcelain is fired at a high temperature and is called "full-bodied," meaning its color is solid throughout the tile. Ceramic tile by comparison is fired at a lower temperature, can be more brittle, and its glaze is on the surface. Both have advantages, from porcelain's ability to withstand chipping to ceramic's ease in cutting for installation.

Ready to tackle installing tile? It's not a task for the nervous. Perhaps you should start small with a bathroom floor. One of my clients balked at the price an installer wanted for tiling a small bathroom and decided to try it himself. He set aside a weekend for the job and went at the task the same way he does everything—full bore. He looked at several books on the subject at his local home improvement store, finally buying Michael Byrne's *Setting Tile*. The book became his bible on tile installation. He was so pleased at the way the floor turned out, he went on to do a bigger room before tiling the backsplash in his kitchen. Who knows what tile project he'll turn to next?

ELSEWHERE ON THE WEB

▶ One of the biggest challenges of a do-it-yourself tiling project consists of buying the right amount of tile and then some, before you even start setting the tile. There's nothing worse than getting 90 percent of the way through a job only to find you don't have enough to finish—and your tile is out of production. This situation is not uncommon. For invaluable instructions on measuring and buying tile, read the Tile Tool at www.ceramic-tile-floor.info/te/tile-tools/tileEstimator-tt.html.

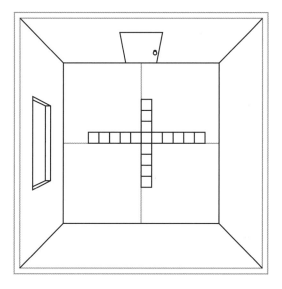

▲ How to begin laying tile

Look upon a tile installation job as a project best performed in careful steps. First, measure properly so that you order enough tiles. Order at least 10 percent more than you need to cover any

▶ Even if you're ready to tackle the installation of a tile floor or wall, don't jump right in. Spend some time reading tips from the experts. *Setting Tile* by Michael Byrne (my previously mentioned client's bible) is a good starting place. It has so much information, you might not need any other source. Tile manufacturers have Web sites with videos that guide you through the steps of tile laying, cutting, placing, and grouting.

breakage or miss-cuts. Also order extras of all other materials you'll be using, such as thinset mortar, spacers, and grout. Believe me, I have heard many horror stories of homeowners running out of tile and being unable to get more because the store is closed. Dye lots can vary, so buying in stages risks getting tile that doesn't look like the rest of the flooring. With such a delay you can run out of energy and enthusiasm, so that you never finish the project.

The next step is where careful planning pays off. One way you can tell a poorly done tile floor is by tile that seems a little crooked, its lines off. To prevent this, it's important to measure the floor and lay a grid pattern by popping a chalk line. I've watched how tile installers spend time at the outset laying that pattern. Some work from the center tile outwards, others from the corner of the room with the longest and straightest walls. Start with a small project, maybe the guest bath; lay a grid pattern and see how that works for you. The best tile installer I've ever watched first laid out every tile in the room, then lifted away a row or two of tile to apply the thinset mortar.

▲ How to spread thinset mortar

Follow package directions carefully to mix the thinset mortar. It should be about the consistency of peanut butter. Apply the mortar to the tile with a trowel and spread it evenly all the way out to the edge. Then set the tile in place. This method works best for beginners, resulting in a flatter, more professional looking floor. It will also keep the mortar from drying too quickly, which is also important for a beginner. If you work carefully, you won't make mistakes or lose confidence. Most beginners need to use spacers to keep the tiles evenly spaced. (One tile installer used pennies instead of little plastic spacers.)

Time for **grout**. As you work to set the tile, be sure not to let too much thinset well up in the channels between the tiles. Occasionally use a pencil to clear these out so you can pour the grout into them. Be sure to allow the mortar to dry according to package directions. Now it's time to mix the grout and apply. Swirling on the grout with a **grout float** is like frosting a cake.

Allow your grout to set for fifteen minutes before wiping the floor clean. Stay off the floor until it has a chance to dry completely—usually at least twenty-four hours. It's important to seal the grout once it is completely dry. Check the label on your sealer, asking the expert at the home improvement store when to apply the product and whether to use one or more coats. Now doesn't that new floor look great?

One of the hottest trends in flooring in recent years is concrete. If you haven't seen one of these new floors, I urge you to give it a look. Often stained and polished, they look incredibly contemporary, not at all a cheap alternative to flooring. I recommend that you get your contractor to do this type of floor when you're building because it's more difficult to install later.

WHAT'S HOT

▶ To make a boring concrete floor the center of attention, paint an interesting pattern. Use stencils or draw freehand a special design on the floor, then carefully paint with floor paint in your chosen colors. Faux paint black-and-white marble tiles, sponge paint a Venetian plaster look, or paint an "area rug" on the concrete. This may seem like a big project, but you'll find that it's not so hard. And you'll save a lot of money over installing tile.

If you already have a concrete floor that needs updating, start by cleaning and drying it thoroughly. It will probably be next to impossible to get it perfectly clean and uniform in color, but do your best. Fill any cracks with resin filler. If you want an interesting focal point on the floor, clean out the cracks, lay colorful pebbles in the cracks, and fill with resin. Then plan to paint the concrete with paint made especially for flooring. (Don't paint yourself into a corner!) Choose a neutral color to blend with any décor or select a pattern or faux finish that will really stand out. Seal the concrete carefully when you're done.

Carpeting: A Soft Touch

Is there anything better than sinking your toes into a soft, cushy rug? Whether wall-to-wall carpet or a large room-sized rug, carpeting can transform a room, adding color, texture, warmth, and comfort. Carpeting has been a traditional floor covering for so many years that it's hard to imagine there was ever a time when people didn't have it. But it hasn't been that long since carpet became a popular floor covering—and an affordable option. Considering that wall-to-wall carpeting is measured, ordered, and installed in different sizes in different rooms of your house, it's actually a custom feature.

I like to use carpeting to add color to a room. Even if you don't want to use a vivid color like red, you don't have to stick to just a few neutral colors to carpet a room. Warm up a living or family room with earth tones, for instance. Although many people like to use the same color of carpeting throughout a house to create a flow, there is no rule that says you have to do so. Adding color in your bedrooms will create a decorating style that is uniquely yours. Install a soft blue carpet in a master bedroom, let your child pick a color she loves for her bedroom carpeting. When you're ready for a change, it's not expensive to replace the carpeting in smaller bedrooms.

Almost nothing sells a house faster than installing new carpeting or flooring. Select neutral colors in carpeting if reselling your home is a consideration. This means warm beiges and cool grays rather than oranges, bright pinks, and purples.

Carpeting is an excellent way to add warmth to a room. If you have small children, especially toddlers just learning to walk, carpeting offers ideal protection compared to hard flooring. You will also appreciate carpeting for its sound-deadening qualities. Those who walk a lot around the house also benefit from the soft surface of carpeting. Even though most people change their carpet every seven to eight years, top-quality carpet lasts far longer, even in high-traffic areas. Carpeting made of man-made fibers has joined traditional materials like wool in long-wearing ability, and stain-resistant treatments have made frequent replacing of carpeting a thing of the past.

There are many different types of carpeting. Here's a list of the most popular:

- **Loop Carpet:** Uncut, level loops of yarn create a level, durable carpet.
- **Cut Pile:** Looped carpet fibers are cut at the top to create a soft, plush effect.
- **Multi-Level Loop:** Different heights of loops create different textures and patterns.
- **Saxony:** Firmly twisted tufts of heavy yarn softened with heat create a very soft texture.
- **Plush or Velvet:** Lightly twisted tufts of fiber have a uniform surface, creating a softer, more level carpet than found in textured carpets.

ASK YOUR GUIDE

I'm getting ready to sell my house, and the carpet is a mess. Any suggestions?

▶ You need to look for the best carpet you can get for the lowest price. Find a balance between skimping and spending more than necessary. Who knows? Your buyer may prefer hardwood floors to carpet and plan to tear out your new carpeting right away. At the same time, you do want your house to look its best for showing.

- **Cable:** Made of very soft and thick twisted yarns.
- **Berber:** Thick strands of yarn are looped to create a tight, rounded surface.

ELSEWHERE ON THE WEB

▶ New carpet for your home is a big investment, one you'll live with for a long time. For extensive information on fibers used in carpets and their particular characteristics, carpet construction, styles of carpet, loop versus plush, density, carpet backing, padding, measuring, and installation, visit the Web site at http://edis.ifas.ufl.edu/HE784. This site from the University of Florida Extension Division covers just about everything you need to know before you go shopping.

Carpet price even on the same brand and style can differ widely from one store to another. Some dealers have a flat per yard rate that includes installation, while others will charge for a number of services you thought were included in the price. It's best (and sometimes required by the dealer) to have a store representative come out to your house and measure. Be sure to ask if that service is free; sometimes it isn't. Is there any charge for moving furniture? How long will the job take? Does the store guarantee installation at the agreed-upon time? Will you need new padding under the new carpeting? Will the installers haul away the old carpeting and related trash? Some cities charge for extra garbage, particularly what looks like renovation debris, so it's important to find out if you can save on this charge (or at least have the old carpeting removed).

Get a written estimate of the cost and a copy of the guarantee for the carpeting plus any stain-resistant finish. I also recommend that my clients get a piece of the carpet and padding they have ordered to make certain they are getting what they've paid for. Who wants a bait-and-switch when you're spending so much money?

Carpeting comes in many colors, styles, and fabrics. But before you choose a color, decide what type of carpet you want and what kind of pad. Why do you need to worry about a pad choice before a color choice? Because the quality of the pad affects the carpet's look and durability. Check on the price and quality of the padding (as well as the carpet) to make an informed choice. Don't skimp on the pad or the installation.

Is the potential traffic in the area you're carpeting high or low? A large, active family has different requirements for carpeting than a couple. Will food be in the room being carpeted (and dropped on it)? Is anyone in your home allergic to certain materials, such as wool? Man-made fibers are now able to withstand almost any challenge of wear and tear. If you have pets, be sure to tell your carpet salesperson. Some carpeting is treated not only for stains but to soak up pet urine that could ruin the carpet and padding.

As with paint, carpet can take on an entirely different color depending on changing light levels in a room. Ask if you can bring home samples, and make sure they're large enough to get a good idea of the color; as with paint chips, it's too hard to make choices from little swatches of carpet.

Ask yourself several questions when you're trying to decide on a carpet. Do you want the carpet to be a neutral backdrop or a color accent? Do you want to use the same color throughout the house? What type of carpet (such as Berber or plush) do you like best? Is the color one you can live with for a long time? How much are you willing to spend on carpeting? You can find it for $5 a square yard to over $50 per square yard. Practical considerations—like the amount of wear and tear it will undergo and your budget—should determine the carpet you choose as much as decorative concerns.

Consider carpet care. A big consideration, especially if the carpeting is in a high traffic area, is how much care it will need. No one wants to vacuum every day or have to clean the carpet every few months, whether with a home shampooer or a professional carpet cleaning company. If your home is small and you can manage it, it might be worth the investment to get your own carpet cleaning machine. They've become lighter and easier to use, and the price is very reasonable when you factor in the inconvenience of lugging one from a rental place back and forth in your car. That way no one

TOOLS YOU NEED

▶ Home carpet cleaning machines have vastly improved in recent years. Older styles squirted water and shampoo onto carpet, scrubbed it around, and left the shampoo in the carpet, creating a dirt magnet for any area you cleaned. New cleaners such as the Hoover SteamVac Dual V work as well as professional cleanings. It automatically mixes hot water and shampoo, injects solution into the carpet, scrubs the dirt, rinses, then sucks the dirt, water, and shampoo into a holding tank.

else has used it but you, so you don't have to first obsessively clean the machine of another household's pet hairs.

One client contacted me when she was buying an older home. The carpet was very dirty and made her sneeze just to walk on it to measure floors and room sizes. But she couldn't afford new carpeting right away. We discovered there was concrete beneath the carpeting, not a wood floor like we'd hoped. We got an estimate to have the carpet double-cleaned and a deodorizing agent sprayed on it. My client immediately stopped sneezing, even before the carpet dried. I had my doubts about how clean the carpet would become, but I was wrong; it looked nearly new. Six months later she had the full cleaning process repeated, and then a year after she'd moved in she was able to afford new carpeting. That's when we got together again and picked out new carpeting for her home.

Area Rugs

A decorative rug that is smaller than a room's size is one of the most versatile decorating items you can have in your home. It's a colorful accent, serves as an anchoring element for a furniture grouping that sets it apart, and also provides texture for your room. Some people can't have carpet because they have pets or allergies, and area rugs are perfect for them. Area rugs range from inexpensive woven rugs of sea grass and other natural fibers to pricey Persians. Using an area rug to further the decorating scheme of a room, I anchor a contemporary sofa, chairs, and coffee table with a patterned rug of bold colors and shapes, use a rag rug in a country kitchen, and a rug with cars and trucks for a little boy's room.

Why not try a rug with a decorating theme? There is a collection of rugs called Gee's Bend by Kathy Ireland made from

ELSEWHERE ON THE WEB

▶ Making a hooked rug is a satisfying quiet-time activity to do throughout the year. And you'll enjoy the results of your work for years to come. Deanne Fitzpatrick (www.hookingrugs.com/newkitpage.html) offers complete kits of wonderful scenes of a simpler life. Claire Murray's designs lean toward New England sights. Both companies provide all the materials necessary to create an heirloom rug. Choose a design to enhance your room, and you'll feel proud every time you see it.

reproduction African-American country quilts, and a collection of Frank Lloyd Wright rugs for Craftsman-style homes. You have a decorating theme? Check rug stores and surf the Internet to find hundreds of areas rugs to match it.

If you like to craft, you might think about hooking your own rug. Claire Murray (www.clairemurray.com) sells charming hand-hooked rugs with flora and fauna that you can buy as kits and complete yourself.

You might be wondering how to clean area rugs. Some area rugs are small enough and washable that they can be tossed right in the washing machine and dryer. Others have to be professionally cleaned. Look at the label before you buy. Vacuum the rug to keep it free of dust and grit that can damage the fibers. If the rug is used on a tile or wood surface and slides around, put some special tape or a rubber waffle pad under it to prevent slipping.

If your area rug is especially valuable, such as a rug passed down in the family or an expensive or rare Persian, be sure to consult a rug cleaning expert so you don't ruin the rug with the wrong cleaner. First try the cleaner on a small patch or corner of the rug on the back. If the cleaner should bleach or damage the rug, the spot will not be noticed. If the cleaner works properly, you can proceed with the rest of the rug.

Accent rugs are a bright decorative touch. Think about putting a patterned rug such as a Persian under your dining room table to add drama. Don't be afraid to put an area rug on top of carpeting; it's a decorating trick. And speaking of tricks, sometimes people put area rugs over something they want to hide, like a damaged piece of wood, a cracked tile, or a puppy stain that won't come out of the carpet.

▶ Instead of bringing back a lot of cheap souvenirs from a trip, think about coming home with a real piece of art. You can't go to a Middle Eastern or Asian country without your senses being saturated with beautiful rugs (and those who are persistent at selling them). I brought a small suitcase inside a larger one when I went to Morocco and came home with a rug for my family room.

Area rugs are nice next to your bed to avoid stepping onto a cold floor first thing in the morning. And think of hanging an especially beautiful area or accent rug as a wall hanging. I've done that several times, to striking effect—and often it's not as expensive as a painting.

Get Linked

Flooring is an important part of decorating a room. You'll find more information on my About.com site.

QUICK TIPS FOR CLEANING HARDWOOD FLOORS

With proper care your hardwood floors will look beautiful for years. Get helpful tips here.
http://about.com/interiordec/cleanhardwood
↗

HOW TO REPAIR CRUSHED CARPET

You notice it when you move furniture—those unsightly dents in the carpet. These tips will help level out the carpet and make it look new.
http://about.com/interiordec/crushedcarpet
↗

COLORFUL KIDS' RUGS

Add color and fun to the floor in a child's room with a themed rug.
http://about.com/interiordec/kidsrugs
↗

Chapter 15

Finishing Touches

What's Missing?

You've now done the hard work of budgeting, buying and hauling home supplies, getting dirty and paint-smeared, and tiring of excuses from contractors. It's time to buy those final accessories that truly put the finishing touches on your home.

Dig down in your decorating file to see what else you need to complete the room you're working on. Maybe you've put in a new floor and bought new furniture for your dining room. New curtains are up, the best china is in the cabinet, and the room is nearly perfect. Nearly. What's missing? It could be lighting. It could be artwork. It could be some special architectural touches like molding. Perhaps your room needs a little luxury to set it apart.

Sometimes a room doesn't feel finished to us because even though we've done major work on it, our personality has been left out. In an effort to contain clutter or because we're trying for a minimalist look, we pack away too many of our books, our knickknacks, our framed photos. We're going to start anew, we think.

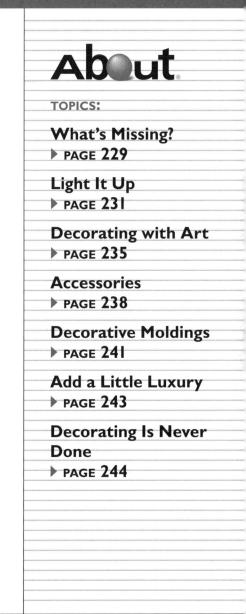

I've been working on my kitchen for months, and everything's done according to plan. But it just feels empty. What have I forgotten?

▶ Even though a kitchen is a workspace, sometimes we forget to dress it up. Look around for objects that add pizzazz to the space. An interesting wreath, a painting or print on the wall, a collection of rolling pins or old kitchen tools contribute interest to the space. Keep looking. You're never really done.

Then we end up with an empty new room that's just a blink away from sterile. A really wonderful room shouldn't look like pages out of a decorating magazine. A room should look lived in. Loved. It should be a visual expression of who we are.

A wonderful room takes time to decorate. We live in a culture of immediate gratification. We watch decorating shows on which people change a room in a few days—or a few hours. A big chain of furniture stores was started on the premise that you can buy an entire room of furniture all in one package, from sofa to side tables to lamps. We shop with our charge cards and acquire what we want right now. But the best decorated rooms take more than a few days to come together. They might take a week, a month, a lifetime. Why rush when you're enjoying simply living in your home? Adding special objects now and then should be a joy, not a race for a quick fix to our home.

Expand on your decorating theme. Everyone loves something, from travel to sports, books to movies or gardening. When you started decorating your home—whether you were doing a minor redecorating or a major remodeling—you picked out furnishings that you liked. You selected colors, fabrics, furniture, and flooring. Now it's time to look at what's still missing. You may be thinking that you've already worked hard decorating and sweated over physically demanding tasks. Maybe your pocketbook is rather empty right now. But the finishing touches don't have to be expensive, and they really will make your room the shining jewel you've imagined.

First look at the pieces you've removed from the room. Did you feel you had to put away all of your collections, your photos, your artwork to make a change? Maybe you're missing those things now. True, some of those items might not be appropriate in your new space. If you changed from a country-themed room to a contemporary room, previous pieces might not look right in your new room. But you can find a new home for your photos by reframing them to better suit your new look. Some glossy black photo frames might set them off and make them fit perfectly in your new contemporary room. Set some of your favorite collectibles around the books in your bookshelves. They might fit in better than you think. Just be sure those collectibles aren't sports memorabilia better suited to a family or great room than the dramatic new contemporary room you've designed.

Light It Up

Nothing sets off a room like good lighting. I've found that so many American homes just have a single fixture (and not a very attractive one) hanging from the center of the ceiling in each room. Then people buy a few inexpensive lamps from a department store with a limited selection. They're seldom changed for years—yet we wonder why we get bored when we walk into a room.

I advise homeowners to pay close attention to the lighting in model homes, designer houses, decorating magazines, and the homes of their friends and families. Go online and look not only at decorating Web sites but also at the many lighting businesses. You'll pick up ideas for your own home. Spend time on lighting choices, and I think you will see what a difference new lighting makes in your home.

Check out track lighting. It's come a long way since the clunky tracks and heads of yesterday. Power now runs to each light head that is clipped to the track. The heads can then be rotated to focus light where you want it, each pointing in a different direction if you like. Today's track lighting is contemporary, easy to install, and some models can be customized to include very interesting fixtures.

WHAT'S HOT

▶ I have a couple of friends who plan trips around shopping for their homes. They went to New Orleans and Charleston to look for interesting wrought iron and England for a set of china. In Provence they sought charming fabrics for a family room, in Germany pewter pieces. They don't spend a lot of money. But they've found some wonderful pieces, inspired by their temporary surroundings. Consider making a visit to a neighboring town where beautiful pottery is made.

▶ Track lighting fixtures come in wonderfully varied sizes and shapes. I've seen fixtures that look like dragonflies, flowers, and shapes that a Murano glassmaker blew. A lighting system with such decorator fixtures gives you a custom system that enhances a room's functionality as well as its beauty. Buy all the parts for your track lighting project from one manufacturer because components are not always interchangeable.

I like track lighting for its versatility—it's flexible in sizing, placement, and fixture styles. Track lighting isn't designed to be general lighting in a room but rather an enhancement, focusing light on specific places you need it most. The light fixtures can be aimed at artwork, kitchen countertops, bookcases, or display cases, at any number of areas to make a dramatic lighting statement. Track lighting looks best in contemporary decorating schemes. It isn't for the traditional or formal room.

Placing track lighting is easy, especially if you have an existing electrical box in the ceiling but need lighting around the room, not just in the center. For best effect, install a track 20" to 40" out from the walls of a room. With higher ceilings track units can be dropped from a central electrical box location. Be sure that track heads don't interfere with your doors, cabinets, or other moving elements in your room.

Imagine having light aimed right where you need it for any task in a room. My clients who have decided to try track lighting at my urging say they don't know what they did without it. Run a straight track along a hallway ceiling for more effective lighting and to showcase artwork on the walls. Customize a track for your specific kitchen needs. If you have an island, you'll want to curve the lighting above it in a U-shaped configuration to help you work better and simultaneously help your children do homework as you cook. Do you have a large closet, particularly a walk-in closet? Install track lighting so you can more easily see what you have.

Installing lighting might be occasion to call in the professionals. Be sure to get advice from an experienced electrical salesperson who knows what kind of connectors, heads, track, and other parts you need for your track lighting project. Check, too, to see whether you'll need a building permit. If light fixture installation is beyond your skill level or you're uncomfortable working with electricity, have the track lights installed by a qualified electrician.

Think about the type of bulb you want before you choose the heads and tracks for your system. All-purpose bulbs like line voltage halogen lamps (also known as PAR lamps) are good for most applications. MR16s (also known as low-voltage halogen) are often used for accent lighting. They require transformers either on each fixture head or installed in the ceiling.

Recessed lights are another contemporary option. It's no wonder recessed lighting has become so popular. It's clean, streamlined, and lights up a room from above. Installing this type of lighting modernizes any room because light opens up a room. Overhead fixtures, table lamps, and floor lamps create pools of light and surrounding shadows. Recessed lighting by contrast sends down light from above with an effect like soft sunlight, seeming to create space and brightness.

Decide how much light you want, then check with a lighting specialist to find out how many fixtures you should install and where to place them for best effect. It's preferable not to put the fixtures too close together or place them in rows, which might make you feel like you're on an airport runway. Think about areas of the room where you read, do special tasks, or have artwork and then place your fixtures to light them. Fireplaces, artwork, sculptures, and flower arrangements all look best when several fixtures light them from different angles. That way they don't look like they're the focus of a spotlight on stage.

Although any room looks bigger when it's well lit, if you want to make a small room feel bigger, install recessed lighting. I like to install wall-washing fixtures (can lights that can be directed around the perimeter of a room to help push the walls out. If you try it, you'll be surprised at how much bigger your room looks. For small rooms install 4" fixtures and use 4" to 6" fixtures in other rooms. The 6" fixtures are good for tall entryways or two-story hallways.

Lights have three parts: the wire that carries the voltage, the fixture, and the bulb. There are two kinds of wire—line voltage (standard Romex) and low voltage. Line voltage can be connected to an incandescent fixture (which uses a standard bulb) or to a fluorescent fixture (which uses a fluorescent bulb). Low-voltage wires run to halogen fixtures (which use halogen bulbs). Incandescent fixtures are inexpensive and good for general light or wall washing. Halogen, which gives a clean white light, comes in flood and spot types. Low-voltage halogen bulbs have a long life and provide more light than incandescent bulbs.

Recessed lighting, which comes in incandescent and halogen, can be used in most homes, unless you have ceilings of concrete or ornate plasterwork. It's important to make sure your recessed lighting is rated for use with any ceiling insulation present.

There are other ways to modernize the lighting in your home. If you don't have the budget or preference for track or recessed lighting, there are some simple things you can do to make your lighting more modern. Install dimmer switches on as many lamps and light fixtures as you can. Dimmed light is soothing in a bathroom when you're taking a bubble bath and romantic in a bedroom. Dimmers not only control the intensity of light, they also save money. For task lighting, install under-cabinet light strips in work areas like the kitchen, your desk area, and your workroom. Be sure every room in your home has a light connected to a dimming wall switch near the entrance that you can turn on when you walk into a room. Then adjust the lighting as you move further into the room.

Lighting on a small scale can make a big difference. Think about putting rope lighting or under-cabinet lights on shelves and in bookcases. Put a small lamp on a bookshelf not only for decoration

▶ Recessed lighting can really make a difference in a kitchen. Nothing modernizes a room more than getting rid of a clunky, outdated fluorescent fixture that casts its ghastly light over many kitchens in older homes. Some homeowners have the skills to remove an old fluorescent fixture and install new recessed lighting. If this is beyond your ability, hire someone to do the work. You'll be glad you did.

but also to break up the line of books. Love to read in bed? If you have small bedside tables, think about adding reading lights on either side of the bed. Also put one near an armchair for pleasant reading there. Old lamps can look new with fresh new shades. It's easy to forget without a lamp in front of you what type and size of lampshade you need, so either take the lamp with you when you visit the lighting store or measure carefully across its top, bottom, and from top to bottom. Also draw a picture. Having the lamp with you offers the opportunity to try out the new shade collections in the store.

Also take a look at uplights, inexpensive fixtures that need only a simple plug-in. They come in metal cans or as small adjustable halogen fixtures. Just place them and then point the light in the direction you want. Designers love to put them on the floor behind a plant, on top of an armoire, or behind furniture to cast a pool of light on a wall. They look good for very little money. Caution: Setting uplights on the floor is not a good idea if you have small children or pets.

Decorating with Art

I love decorating with art. You can express your personality beautifully with a few well-chosen paintings, prints, or photographs, spending a little or a lot. Taste in art is subjective; what one person loves, another may not. If you love a particular work, feel free to enjoy it in your own home. Don't feel you have to hang a Monet print if it's too tame for you or put up something contemporary if you prefer French country landscapes.

Perhaps you like photos more than paintings. I have a friend who in recent years has chosen to exhibit black-and-white photographs rather than paintings in her home, which is decorated in minimalist style. She prefers to reserve bursts of color for pillows tossed on her black sofa rather than through paintings on the walls.

ELSEWHERE ON THE WEB

▶ Since no lighting store can display every light fixture available, most focus on styles favored by the majority of local buyers. Go online to view large selections of fixture styles. A company I use frequently is Murray-Feiss (http://feiss.com). Their fixtures are classic yet stylish, well-made, and artistic.

Try this designer trick to determine whether a painting is the right size for a space. Cut a piece of wrapping paper or newspaper to the size of your artwork and tape to the wall with masking tape. Does it seem the right size? Is the placement right? Before you hammer in a nail, ask someone to hold the painting in place for you and to move it around until it's in the right spot.

Stumped by how high to hang your artwork? A general rule is to hang artwork so that the center of the painting or grouping is at eye level for a person of average height. Another rule is to never hang an artwork over a piece of furniture less wide. Try to keep artwork in 75-percent proportion to a furniture arrangement. Group small pictures in narrow spaces like hallways, saving artwork for more commanding areas like over a sofa or a mantel.

▲ A large piece of artwork centered above a couch.

Try hanging a grouping of pictures or photos. Arranging a grouping on the wall needn't be an intimidating process. To avoid photos tilting in every direction and nail holes everywhere, lay the pictures out on the floor first. Then move these around until you get the look you want. Cut paper in the shapes of the pictures and place the cutouts on the wall with masking tape. These will let you know whether the arrangement works and guide you in hammering the nails for the picture hangers.

There are special considerations in hanging artwork. In scaled-down homes it can be tricky to hang artwork. This doesn't mean, however, that you have to scale down the sizes of your pictures. Just as several large pieces of furniture sometimes serve to make a small space look bigger, so too will one big piece of artwork enhance a small room. Usually a sofa doesn't look right with just a small picture above it and needs a big overhead artwork to add focus to a room.

Do you have a room without a view? Put up paintings or photos that bring a view inside. Shoot photos of your neighborhood and sites that you love in your city. Try for interesting shots, unusual angles, and eye-catching subjects. Don't worry about now being a professional photographer; the new digital cameras facilitate the process. Have the images enlarged to a size that will enhance your space.

Watching your budget? Calendars offer art that you can cut out and frame inexpensively. Or get inspired by Mother Nature and mount pressed flowers, leaves, and shells in a shadow box. Use white glue or spray adhesive for small items and hot glue and a heavier mat for weightier pieces.

ASK YOUR GUIDE

I have a set of china from my grandmother that is too old to use every day. What can I do with the pieces?

▶ If you have a collection of interesting plates, create a decorative display. I purchased some beautiful plates on several trips to France and hung them in my bedroom. Family heirloom china, beautifully painted, hangs on the wall in my dining room. The round and oval shapes add interest when grouped with rectangular and square artwork.

Accessories

Accessories like mirrors, architectural elements, baskets, candles, and clocks are finishing touches that add personality to a room. These don't have to cost a lot of money. Exhibit objects brought back from travels and items from crafts stores.

Keep an eye out for finishing touches in designer houses, model homes, decorating magazines and catalogs, and furnishing stores. For an ethnic-style living room, include an African sculpture you found in an import store or a Japanese porcelain tea set from an Asian goods store. Group a collection of figurines atop your fireplace mantel or tuck these in a bookcase in the living room. A client who bought a small lighthouse object ended up with a collection after family and friends gave her these accessories as gifts. The collection can in turn set a decorating theme for an entire room.

Mirrors, as noted earlier, are wonderful finishing touches. Large mirrors set in striking frames add drama to a room. Small mirrors can be grouped for a charming effect. Even mirrors used for utilitarian purposes such as over a bathroom sink needn't look boring. Paint a plain mirror frame or glue shells on little ornaments like shells before mounting it in your bathroom. Hang a mirror with a big velvet ribbon for a rich look. Include mirrors in varying shapes over a fireplace to reflect natural light. Just be sure your mirror reflects a pleasing view. A mirror hung opposite a window gives the appearance of a second window. Reflect an interesting architectural feature in a mirror to lend balance to a room. A mirror in a dining room makes diners feel special, like they're dining out.

Candles are great for creating a mood in a room. So many people love to decorate with candles because they're generally inexpensive, they're very versatile, and they come in lots of fun varieties. You can choose just about any size, type, color, and scent

ELSEWHERE ON THE WEB

▶ Arranging collections on a table top or in a bookcase is much like preparing a party setting. A number of Web sites sell "tablescapes," which consist of table settings arranged with decorative elements. A Web site called A Tablescape (www.atablescape.com/Main.htm) offers a gallery of party and special-occasion settings to inspire decorative tables. Tablescaping (a new entry in the 2006 Oxford Dictionary), is discussed at Touch of France (www.touchoffrance.com/table_scapes.html).

you can imagine—from tall, slender white candlesticks for an elegant dinner table to small colorful votives as an extra touch for a bathroom or bedroom. You can even find candles made from materials other than traditional wax these days. For example, soy candles are quickly growing in popularity due to the fact that they burn cleaner than traditional wax candles.

Don't forget that part of the fun of decorating with candles is choosing the candleholders! You can find countless variations at home goods stores, department stores, and specialty shops, and you can even use found objects as candleholders for a unique look. Place candles in clean, empty mason jars for a rustic room, or arrange a bunch on a plate or tray for use as a centerpiece. When it comes to decorating with candles, the sky's the limit.

WHAT'S HOT

▶ A decorative pillow is one of the easiest accessories to sew. Even if you can't incorporate cording, ruffles, or tassels, you can create a piece to add color to a site. Select an interesting fabric or use a pair of napkins, sew the four sides, turn the piece right side out, stuff it with a pillow form, and sew up the opening. There are more instructions for making pillows at http://about.com/interiordec/sewpillows.

▲ A collection of votives as a centerpiece

Decorative pillows also make delightful finishing touches in a room. Mix round and square pillows in contrasting materials like satin, burlap, and wool to add color, shape, and texture to a sofa. Pillows in prints, stripes, and solids work well together. You can trim your pillows with fringe, sequins, and buttons for a festive look. Top a bed with decorative pillows to make it look more inviting. You can frequently and inexpensively update a few tossed pillows on upholstered furniture.

Custom decorative pillows are quite expensive, but it's possible to find bargains. What might seem like an extravagant pillow can go a long way in visually impacting a room for relatively little money. I tell clients wary of trying a strong color in a room to experiment with accessories like pillows.

▲ Decorative pillows

When selecting pillows, be careful to choose sizes, shapes, and textures that are not only decorative but also create a comfortable spot. What's the use of a display of beautiful pillows on a sofa if every one needs to be removed before you sit down? And you have to decide whether eight or ten decorative pillows on top of a bed really make it more comfortable. Perhaps all the pillows just make getting into bed at night and making the bed in the morning more trouble than it's worth. Practicality is always a consideration in decorating.

Decorative Moldings

A number of architectural elements are often overlooked in home decorating. Decorative moldings are one of my favorites. Pieces of molded wood (usually) installed at the intersection of wall and ceiling around a room, **crown molding** is an architectural detail people have fallen in love with in recent years. Old Victorian homes in particular boast molding handmade by wood craftsmen. Molding today is factory-made and sometimes made of molded wood product, resin, or plastic rather than wood.

Molding is a decorative feature that gives a finished look to rooms, whether in contemporary or period homes. It can hide shoddy construction by bridging gaps in wall joints, dress up cabinets and doors, and make a home look a cut above ones similar in style. Pieces of molding range from 3" to 15" in width depending on the size of the room and the style of décor. Although molding near the ceiling is usually painted white (or the same color as the ceiling), I've seen glossy black molding used in a colonial home that was beautiful.

Top ten places to use decorative molding:

- **Around the ceiling:** This is popularly known as crown molding.
- **Around a window:** Called *casing*, it's used to hide the gap between window frame and wall.

ELSEWHERE ON THE WEB

▶ Although installing molding isn't too difficult to tackle yourself, it requires precise cuts and careful placement. Draw a plan on paper, one wall at a time. Determine your budget and decide on the style, design, and quantity of pieces you'll need. The Do-It-Yourself network provides clear instructions on measuring, cutting, and installing decorative molding at www.doityourself.com/stry/h2molding.

▶ Simply adding molding pieces to the front of plain kitchen cabinets has a transformative effect. Sketch the design in proportion on the face of the cabinet doors. Using a miter saw, cut the lengths, taking special care to get the pieces even. Glue and lightly nail the molding pieces on the doors, then paint the cabinets. They look new, don't they? This same technique can also be applied to ordinary doors.

- **Around a door:** Also called casing, this covers gaps in installation between door frame and wall.
- **Along the floor:** Usually called **baseboard**, this molding is applied where wall and floor meet. It's not only decorative but functional, hiding the gap between the two surfaces and protecting the wall from scuff marks.
- **On a door:** Dress up a plain door with molding in the form of panels. This technique can add style to kitchen cabinets.
- **Along a wall:** Called chair rail molding, this is installed horizontally around a wall at chair-height for protection as well as decoration.
- **On a wall:** Create a dramatic wall frame for little money.
- **Framing a bookcase:** Crown molding turns a basic bookcase into beautiful furniture. The pieces can be glued on or nailed. Paint the bookcase and molding all one color for a unified look.
- **On a ceiling:** Today's ceiling medallions are often made of polyurethane foam or polystyrene. They make a dramatic focal point in a formal room while providing a mounting area for a chandelier.
- **Around your fireplace:** Vertical molding frames the sides and horizontal molding forms a mantel. Create a dramatic mantel by displaying treasures and seasonally hanging Christmas stockings.

Choosing moldings. It's important to choose decorative molding based on the architectural style of your home and the room you're decorating. If you have a contemporary home, you'll want sleeker moldings than if you own a period home. Determine the height of crown molding by the size and height of a room. A large room and high ceiling can obviously accommodate larger crown molding than can a small room. Designers like about one inch of molding for every foot of ceiling height. That means a 10' ceiling should use crown molding that's 10" high. However, avoid overpowering a room with molding.

Installation is easier than you think. After measuring carefully, set aside the strips of molding for about ten days before installing. They need to adjust to the room's temperature and humidity conditions before finishing. To cut molding, you'll need a saw and a miter box, a handy box with slotted sides for cutting joints. Or order the "Magic Mitre Kit with Handsaw and Template" from www.qvc.com.

Before installing, prime and paint or stain both sides of the molding. This eliminates the need to paint the pieces while you're standing on a ladder. Let them dry for at least twenty-four hours (longer, if possible) before nailing up the molding. If your molding is thin and light, you can space your nails about a foot or so apart; heavier wood requires more frequently placed nails. Finding a stud first isn't necessary when hammering.

Want to make the molding more distinctive? Apply umber glaze, and then wipe it off. Glaze settles into the crevices, highlighting the molding details. Test the process on a piece of scrap molding first.

Add a Little Luxury

Every home can use a little luxury, something sensuous, rare, and elevated in importance that makes you feel privileged and pampered. A lovely antique is a luxury item, as is something handmade by an artisan or crafted of fine materials like silver and crystal. An object of exceptional design or exquisite detail is a luxury. Museum-quality pieces and authentic designer goods of special value, especially ones with recognized cachet, are also prized luxuries. How can homeowners of average means create an equivalent atmosphere of luxury at home?

ELSEWHERE ON THE WEB

▶ Are you ready for an over-the-top nursery? You can find special items in high-end baby stores, and a fuller selection of luxury baby furniture and accessories is found online. Both Posh Tots (http://poshtots.com) and Bratt Décor (www.bratt decor.com) have custom-built wood and iron cribs, beds, chests, armoires and rockers. Add silk and satin bedding and adorable themed lamps, and your baby's room will be the talk of the town.

Start with accessories that feel special. Even small pleasures can make your home feel luxurious. A friend of mine told me that she upgraded the thread count in her bed sheets every few years so that sliding into her bed every night now feels luxurious. If you can't afford a sofa covered in brocade (which isn't so practical anyway if you have small children and pets), add rich and elegant brocade pillows to your **microfiber** sofa. That antique tea set, a family heirloom residing on the buffet in your dining room, brings enhancing luxury to your home.

Children also enjoy a touch of luxury in their rooms. As families shrink in size while family earning power increases, people are spending money on the bedrooms and playrooms of their children like never before. Major manufacturers feature collections for kids that are truly luxurious. Cinderella coach beds, bassinets and cribs with fancy lace-trimmed canopies, and matching sumptuous bed linens have all found a place in many average-income homes.

Such luxe furnishings have staying power. Furniture sets used for babies can be converted as they grow, some pieces even adapted to a grown child's first apartment. So buying luxury items, which consist of finely made, durable products, can be a matter of good planning.

Decorating Is Never Done

I hope by now you've set to work on your home decorating goals. Do you have a sparkling updated dining room to enjoy with your family? A redesigned master bedroom? Newly styled rooms for the kids? Whatever you've been able to accomplish thus far, give yourself a pat on the back. Home decorating is not always easy, and even if you've just worked through the planning stage by now, you've done a lot.

Although I've been discussing finishing touches in home decorating, I'd like to emphasize that your projects are never completely finished. Just as life is a journey rather than a destination, so is home decorating an ongoing process rather than a final product. The fun of decorating is in perpetually making your home new and fresh. Take on clever new projects to create a home that's warmer, more special, and more suited to you. Keep exploring ways to express your personality in your house. For your home is truly your castle, and the work of turning it into what you want is something to enjoy!

Get Linked

Putting the finishing touches on your home is an ongoing process. Read about more ways to dress up your home at these links on my About. com Interior Decorating site.

ADD YOUR OWN PERSONALITY TO A ROOM

By including furnishings and objects that have special meaning to you, your room will take on a personality of its own.

http://about.com/interiordec/personality

TIPS ON USING DECORATIVE MOLDING

With the simple addition of decorative molding, your room can take on a more elegant look. Learn the basics of using decorative molding in your home.

http://about.com/interiordec/moldingtips

Appendix A

Glossary

antebellum
refers to the time before the Civil War in the United States

armchair
a chair, usually upholstered, with sides on which to rest one's arms

armoire
a tall cabinet, usually with drawers, shelves, and doors, used for storing clothes or household items

ASID
American Society of Interior Designers, an organization of professional interior designers

balloon shade
a window treatment of fabric with deep inverted pleats pulled up with rings and cording that cause the fabric to fall into rounded scallops at the bottom

Better Business Bureau
a network of local organizations whose purpose is to receive and investigate customer complaints of dishonest business practices

bistro set
a dining ensemble, usually a small round table and side chairs

blind
a covering over a window to block light from entering a room (for example, vertical blinds, aluminum blinds, wooden blinds)

brass
a shiny yellow metal made from an alloy of copper and zinc, used for decorative pieces and hardware

budget
a plan defining how time or money is to be spent during a particular period of time

buffet
a piece of furniture usually found in a dining room for holding linens, dishes, and serving pieces

building permit
a written legal document, usually produced by a public entity, giving permission to build in accord with laws and prescribed practices

café curtains
a usually casual style of fabric window treatment that covers only the lower half of a window

caulking
using a waterproof sealer to hold windows in place, seal tile joints, and fill gaps or cracks

chaise lounge

an upholstered couch in the shape of a chair, usually with one arm rest and a long front for resting the legs

chandelier

a hanging light fixture with branches that hold light bulbs or candles

complementary colors

on a color wheel, the color complement created by combining the other two primary colors (for example, the complement of red is green [blue and yellow], the complement of blue is orange [yellow and red], and the complement of yellow is magenta [blue and red]).

contractor

the person responsible for coordinating subcontractors and laborers, schedules, and supplies on a building construction or renovating project

cornice

a decorative wooden box, usually covered with padded fabric, that covers drapery hardware and frames the top of a window

curtains

a usually casual style of fabric window treatment

daybed

a bed or couch used for resting during the day and as a bed at night

denim

a heavyweight woven cotton cloth used for apparel and upholstery

dinette set

a small dining ensemble consisting of a table and chairs and often made of wood, metal, or Formica

drapery or drapes

cloth hanging over a window opening or on a wall

drywall

prefabricated sheets of building material used to create walls by nailing to studs

duvet

a quilt for a bed, usually with a decorative cover

eclectic

drawing from a variety of sources or styles

equity

the difference between the market value of a home and the amount of the mortgage loan held against it

ethnic

related to or associated with the traditional culture traits of a national or social group

fabric swatch

a small piece of fabric or carpet used as a sample

faux

an imitation of a natural finish or material, such as faux painting or faux fur

finial

a decorative ornament at the top of a post or at the end of a drapery rod

flatware

eating utensils, including knives, forks, and spoons

focal point
the center of attention; the place where eyes are drawn to

futon
mattress pad used for sleeping on the floor or on a raised platform

hue
a color or shade of a color (for example, pink is a hue of red)

laminate floor
a flooring surface of man-made material made to look like wood or other more expensive alternatives

loft bed
a bed that is placed on high stilts, leaving room underneath for furniture

louver
one of a set of narrow openings or slats in a door or window that allows in light and air

loveseat
a small sofa or double chair for seating two people

mantel
a decorative frame around a fireplace, usually made of wood, stone, or brick

matchstick blinds
a roll-up window covering usually made of shafts of bamboo or other grasses

memorabilia
collectible items associated with a particular event, place, or occasion

microfiber
very fine strands of fiber woven to create soft and durable fabric for clothing and household goods

mitre box
a box with a template to help you cut specific shapes of wood

mortgage
a written contract between a lender and buyer using real property as collateral

mural
a large painting applied directly on a wall

opaque
not clear; with fabrics, not transmitting light

ottoman
an upholstered stool or bench used for resting feet or placing trays

pewter
a dull gray metal made from an alloy of lead and tin used for decorative tableware and hardware

Phillips head screwdriver
a screwdriver that has an X-shaped point used to install a Phillips screw with an X-shaped tip

primer
an undercoating of paint or sealer used to prepare a surface for a final coat of paint or other finish

rattan
woven stems of plants used to build furniture

Roman shade
a window covering usually of fabric that lowered covers the whole window and raised creates pleats parallel to the floor

secretary

a tall cabinet with a fold-down desktop, a bookcase on top, and drawers below

shutter

a window covering usually of wood with stationary or moveable louvers that close a window

sideboard

a waist-high piece of dining room furniture used to store linens and tableware

sisal

a strong white fiber made from the leaves of the agave plant

slipcover

a removable covering for a piece of upholstered or wooden furniture

soft goods

articles of home décor made of textile or fabric, such as draperies, upholstered or slipcovered furniture, and bedding

strié

striped, usually referring to wall covering, paint finish, or weave of fabric

swag

a piece of fabric draped over a rod at the top of a window

symmetrical

being balanced in size, mass, and position

template

a pattern used to duplicate something

toile

a cotton or linen fabric with a white or natural ground printed with a decorative pattern in one color

trend

a current fashion or style

trundle bed

a low bed on wheels that can be slid under the frame of another bed

valance

an element of a window treatment at the top of a window covering the window frame and hardware

vanity

a cabinet in a bathroom that holds a sink and plumbing, usually with storage underneath and drawers

Appendix B

Room Arrangement Cutouts

Use these cutouts to plan how you're going to arrange different rooms in your home. You may want to photocopy the furniture shapes and then cut them out so you can move them around on the graph paper. Once you've decided on an arrangement, pin them in place. Reuse the cutouts and graph paper for each new reorganization project.

Office Furniture Cutouts

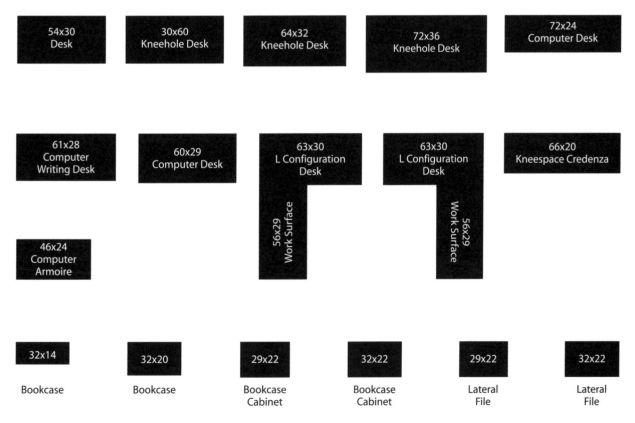

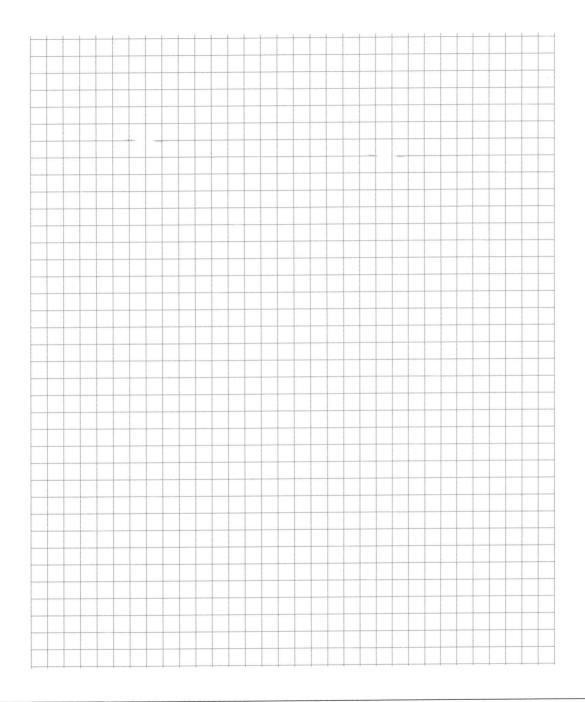

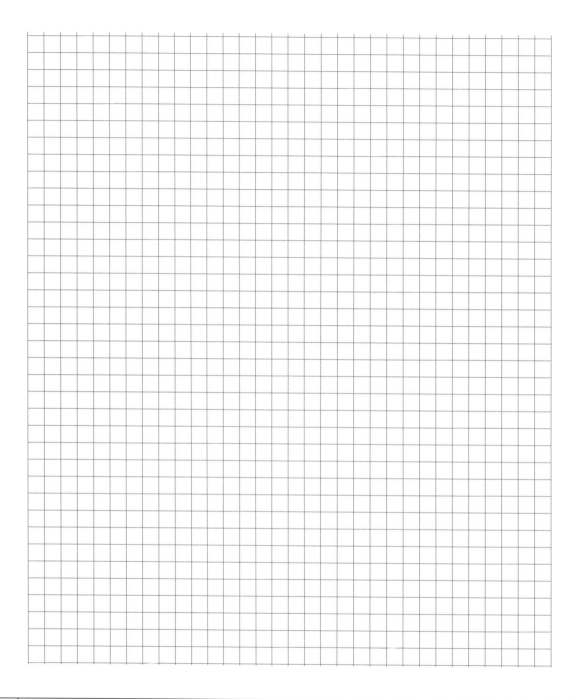

Bedroom Furniture Cutouts

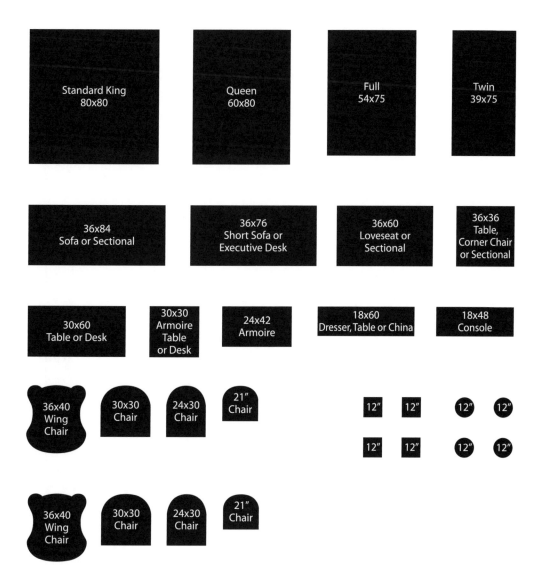

Standard King
80x80

Queen
60x80

Full
54x75

Twin
39x75

36x84
Sofa or Sectional

36x76
Short Sofa or
Executive Desk

36x60
Loveseat or
Sectional

36x36
Table,
Corner Chair
or Sectional

30x60
Table or Desk

30x30
Armoire
Table
or Desk

24x42
Armoire

18x60
Dresser, Table or China

18x48
Console

36x40
Wing
Chair

30x30
Chair

24x30
Chair

21"
Chair

12" 12" 12" 12"

12" 12" 12" 12"

36x40
Wing
Chair

30x30
Chair

24x30
Chair

21"
Chair

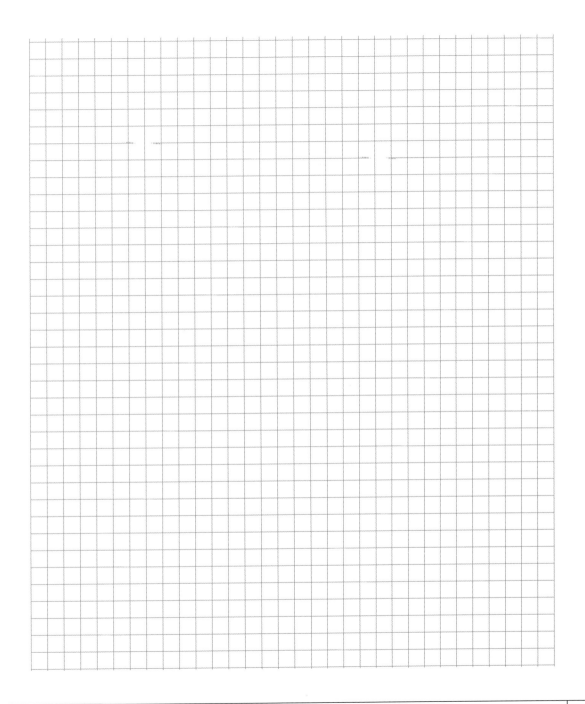

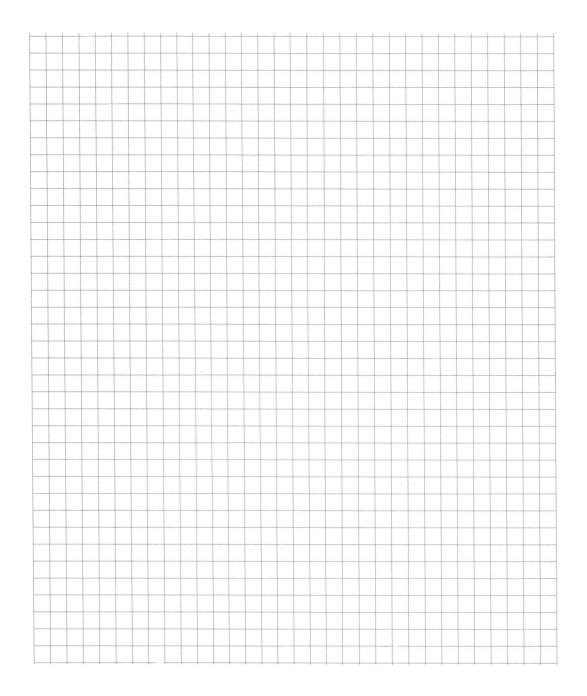

The *ABOUT*.com *Guide to* **Home Decorating**

Living Room Furniture Cutouts

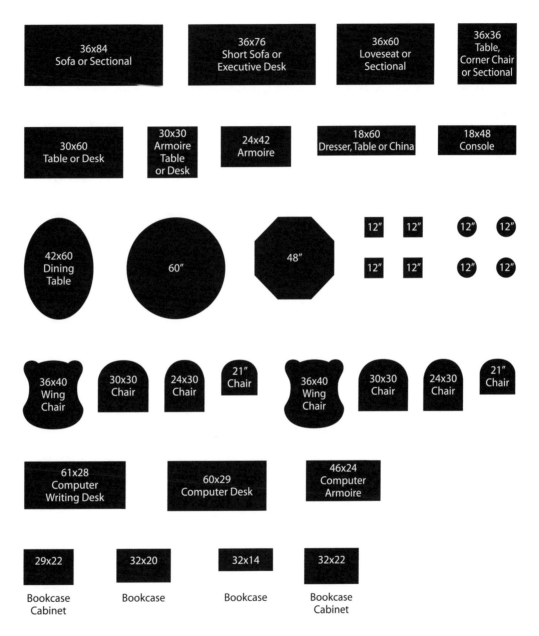

36x84
Sofa or Sectional

36x76
Short Sofa or
Executive Desk

36x60
Loveseat or
Sectional

36x36
Table,
Corner Chair
or Sectional

30x60
Table or Desk

30x30
Armoire
Table
or Desk

24x42
Armoire

18x60
Dresser, Table or China

18x48
Console

42x60
Dining
Table

60"

48"

12" 12" 12" 12"

12" 12" 12" 12"

36x40
Wing
Chair

30x30
Chair

24x30
Chair

21"
Chair

36x40
Wing
Chair

30x30
Chair

24x30
Chair

21"
Chair

61x28
Computer
Writing Desk

60x29
Computer Desk

46x24
Computer
Armoire

29x22

Bookcase
Cabinet

32x20

Bookcase

32x14

Bookcase

32x22

Bookcase
Cabinet

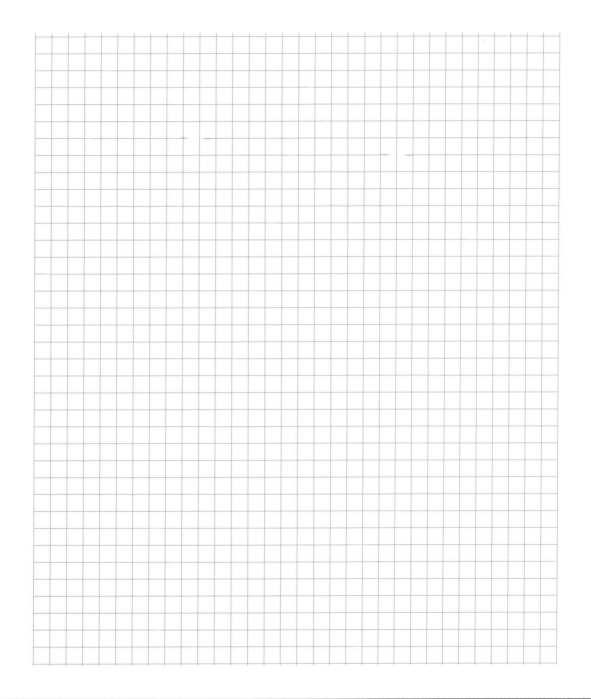

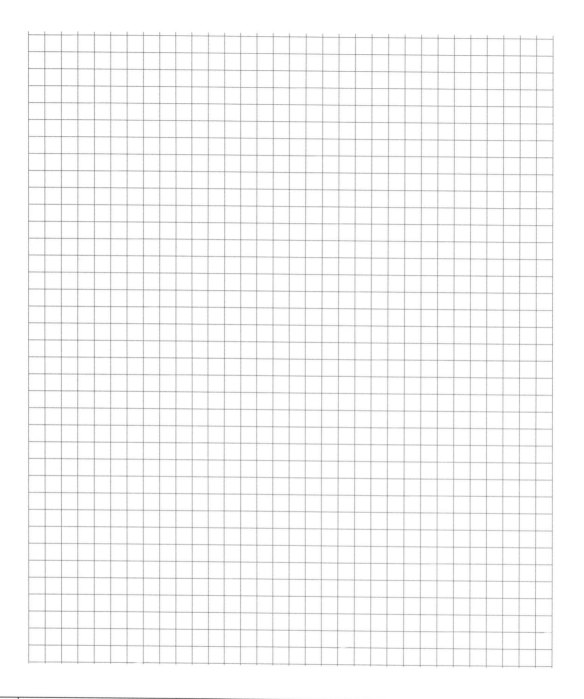

The **ABOUT**.com *Guide to* **Home Decorating**

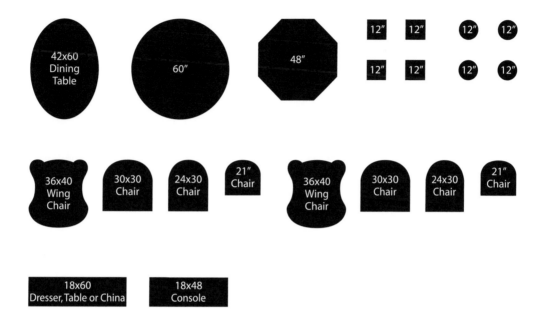

42x60
Dining
Table

60"

48"

12" 12" 12" 12"

12" 12" 12" 12"

36x40
Wing
Chair

30x30
Chair

24x30
Chair

21"
Chair

36x40
Wing
Chair

30x30
Chair

24x30
Chair

21"
Chair

18x60
Dresser, Table or China

18x48
Console

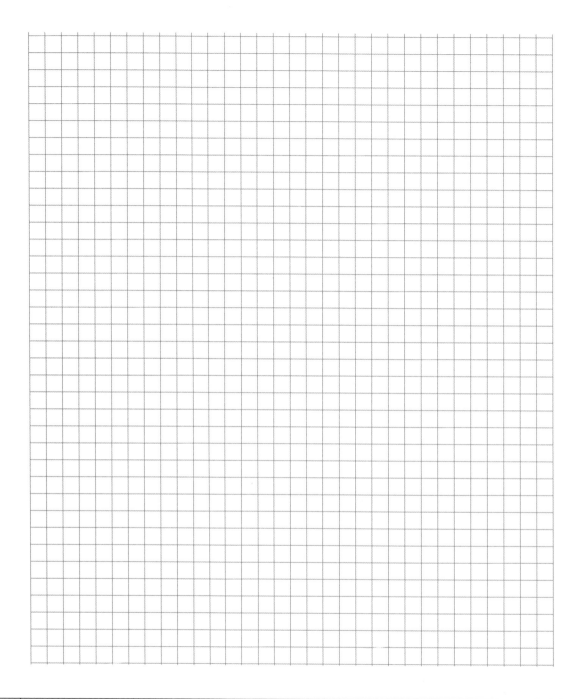

The **ABOUT.com** *Guide to* **Home Decorating**

Appendix C

Other Sites and Further Reading

Web Sites

About.com's site for Furniture

This site offers good resources for furniture, reviews of new releases, buying guides, and helpful decorating information.

http://furniture.about.com

About.com's site for Architecture

Learn about architecture and styles of decorating that developed through the years.

http://architecture.about.com

About.com's site for Home Repair

Find tutorials and help to repair many things in your home, from broken tile to peeling wallpaper to leaking pipes.

http://homerepair.about.com

About.com's site for Home Renovations

Learn the basics and intricacies of home renovation projects.

http://homerenovations.about.com

Better Homes & Gardens

Their house and home section offers articles and pictures on creating beautiful homes and seasonal decorating projects.

http://bhg.com

HGTV

Home and Garden Television Web site provides tutorials and helpful ideas for home decorating and renovation taken from their television shows.

http://hgtv.com

Redecorate.com

Use what you have to transform your space in twenty-four hours with help from interior refiner Laurie Ward.

www.redecorate.com

Do It Yourself

From wiring a light switch to installing wallpaper, this Web site provides instructions for the Do-It-Yourselfer.

www.doityourself.com

Reading

Decorating with a Personal Touch by Alison Wormleighton
Accompanied by beautiful photographs, this book encourages the homeowner to use personal things to create a unique home.

The Impatient Decorator: 201 Shortcuts to a Beautiful Home by Glenna Morton
Read quick tips and valuable suggestions for adding punch and function to a home from About.com's former Guide to Interior Decorating.

Fabrications by Katrin Cargill
A good resource for the home sewer, this book offers over 1,000 ways to decorate your home with fabric.

The Complete Home Decorator by Stewart Walton
Going from room to room and element to element, the author offers 1,000 design ideas for the home.

In Your Own Style: The Art of Creating Wonderful Rooms by Linda Chase and Laura Cerwinske
Read about lighting, flooring, wall coverings, hardware, color, and other resources for creating a beautiful home.

Before & After Decorating from HGTV
Using before and after photographs, HGTV's publication shows easy ways to transform every room of your home.

Complete Home Decorating by Phil Gorton
This book is a step-by-step guide on how to make the most of your home with instructions on installations, painting projects, and repairs.

Shabby Chic by Rachel Ashwell
The diva of transforming trash to treasure defines the shabby chic style in her first book.

Index

Note: **Bold** page references indicate ABOUT.
  com Get Linked information.

▶ IT'S About. *INFORMATION DELIVERED IN A REVOLUTIONARY NEW WAY.*

The Internet. Books. Experts. This is how—and where—we get our information today. And now, the best of these resources are available together in a revolutionary new series of how-to guides from **About.com** and Adams Media.

**The About.com Guide to
Acoustic Guitar**
ISBN 10: 1-59869-098-1
ISBN 13: 978-1-59869-098-9

**The About.com Guide to
Baby Care**
ISBN 10: 1-59869-274-7
ISBN 13: 978-1-59869-274-7

**The About.com Guide to
Getting in Shape**
ISBN 10: 1-59869-278-X
ISBN 13: 978-1-59869-278-5

**The About.com Guide to
Having a Baby**
ISBN 10: 1-59869-095-7
ISBN 13: 978-1-59869-095-8

**The About.com Guide to
Job Searching**
ISBN 10: 1-59869-097-3
ISBN 13: 978-1-59869-097-2

**The About.com Guide to
Owning a Dog**
ISBN 10: 1-59869-279-8
ISBN 13. 978-1-59869-279-2

**The About.com Guide to
Shortcut Cooking**
ISBN 10: 1-59869-273-9
ISBN 13: 978-1-59869-273-0

**The About.com Guide to
Southern Cooking**
ISBN 10: 1-59869-096-5
ISBN 13: 978-1-59869-096-5

Available wherever books are sold! Or call us at 1-800-258-0929 or visit us at *www.adamsmedia.com.*